Long Days, Short Years

Long Days, Short Years

A Cultural History of Modern Parenting

Andrew Bomback

The MIT Press

Cambridge, Massachusetts | London, England

The MIT Press would like to thank the anonymous peer reviewers who provided comments on drafts of this book. The generous work of academic experts is essential for establishing the authority and quality of our publications. We acknowledge with gratitude the contributions of these otherwise uncredited readers.

This book was set in Stone Serif and Stone Sans by Westchester Publishing Services. Printed and bound in the United States of America.

Library of Congress Cataloging-in-Publication Data

Names: Bomback, Andrew, author.
Title: Long days, short years : a cultural history of modern parenting / Andrew Bomback.
Description: Cambridge, Massachusetts : The MIT Press, [2022] | Includes bibliographical references and index.
Identifiers: LCCN 2021047583 | ISBN 9780262047159 (hardcover)
Subjects: LCSH: Parenting, | Child rearing. | Parent and child.
Classification: LCC HQ755.8 .B646 2022 | DDC 649/.1—dc23/eng/20211001
LC record available at https://lccn.loc.gov/2021047583

10   9   8   7   6   5   4   3   2   1

To my family

All the years of ritual—undressing and dressing, diaper changes, potty time, bath time, tooth brushing, reading, hugs and kisses—are so *exhausting*. If they don't fall asleep beside him, whoever is on bedtime duty stumbles downstairs, announces wearily, "And that concludes today's parenting." Until the next day, and the next and the next. As if it were a curse and not a blessing. As if it really were forever.

—Peter Ho Davies, *A Lie Someone Told You About Yourself*

Contents

Author's Note

My neighbor, Frank, a clinical psychologist, recently published his first book, *The Fear Paradox*.[1] In its opening pages, he quotes Franklin Delano Roosevelt's famous lines about the "nameless, unreasoning, unjustified terror that paralyzes needed efforts to convert retreat into advance," primarily to point out that his book does not aim to free its readers from this paralysis. "That is what countless self-help books attempt to free us from," he writes. "But what I have come to wonder about is why fear is so difficult for us in the first place." He advises his readers to approach this material not as a "how to" but rather as a "how come" book.

Over the years, I've borrowed gardening tools, baking ingredients, and bridge tables from my neighbors, and here I'd like to borrow Frank's phrasing. I am in no position to write a "how to" book on raising children. While I am a father, I am not a particularly good one, as I will confess throughout this book. In fact, I set out to write this book because I was struggling so much with my parenting. Years earlier, facing down a midcareer crisis as a physician, I wrote a book dissecting what exactly I and other doctors did each day, hoping to better understand why I'd chosen this profession and figure out whether and how I could continue in the field. I was in a similar crisis when I began writing this book. I knew why I'd chosen parenthood but worried about how I was performing in the task and whether this performance would ever improve. I hoped that analyzing what it meant to be a parent today might give me some insight into what I was doing wrong and what, potentially, I could do right for my family. And I sensed that many other parents were staring down the same question that I was—namely, how come this is so hard?

My book on doctors was called *Doctor*,[2] and I originally titled this book *Parent*. I realize I can be accused of a lack of imagination, but in my mind there was an important distinction between the two titles. I was using *doctor* as a noun and *parent* as a verb. As I will discuss in the forthcoming pages, the verb form of *parent* is a relatively new entry in our collective lexicon, and not a particularly salubrious one. With the exception of chapter 9, this book makes no attempt to dole out advice on how to parent. Throughout, though, I try to address the question of how come it can be so much fun to be a parent and yet so incredibly frustrating to parent.

Parenting is an emotional subject. I expect the vast majority—if not all—of those who read this book will be parents or caregivers with some skin in the game. In some ways, how a reader feels about the subject of parenting, even as an academic topic, cannot be divorced from how a reader feels about their own parenting. I do not intend this to be a controversial book, but I also understand that some of the subject matter may elicit strong reactions. One of my central themes is that anxiety plagues modern parents, which can be a difficult pill to swallow (even if you've read *The Fear Paradox*). I explore this and other themes with reviews of historical trends, dissections of popular culture, interviews with other parents, and, throughout, my own parenting stories. I intend these bits of personal memoir to open up spaces for others to reflect on their own challenges and opportunities as parents. I also intend these stories to highlight how, in my own life, I evaluate parenting with curiosity and respect. I have tried to approach all of the material in this book with that same curiosity and respect.

I recognize that I am not the conventional messenger for this material. I am a physician, but one who specializes in rare kidney disorders in adult patients. I am an academic, but my research is focused primarily on evaluating novel treatments for these rare kidney disorders. Therefore, I have been cognizant throughout the process of creating this book that I am, in many ways, an outsider to the material, despite having a house filled with small children. I have been fortunate to rely on the work of others who are more conventional messengers— particularly two recent histories of parenting, Jennifer

Traig's *Act Natural*[3] and Paula S. Fass's *The End of American Childhood*.[4] I strongly encourage readers to seek out these and other works cited in my endnotes for alternative versions of this subject matter.

I also recognize that I am able to approach this material from a place of privilege. Not only am I a card-carrying member of the WEIRD (Western, Educated, Industrialized, Rich, Democratic) demographic,[5] I also am a white, straight, cisgender, able-bodied man. The WEIRD demographic has both produced and consumed a substantial chunk of the parenting literature, and yet this same demographic–especially WEIRD men—too often view parenting as something that "other" people should do for them. The male voice in the parenting sphere is unusual; when it does appear, it's more likely to tackle the subject from a humorous rather than a serious perspective. While I have intended my analyses to be objective and, save for some specific subject matter (e.g. chapter 5), gender-neutral, I am not naive enough to believe that readers will forget that I am a man writing about a verb with different expectations for moms than dads. I hope that an honest and humble accounting of my efforts to understand this subject matter is the best way to ensure that I am not running the risk of "mansplaining" parenthood. In addition, whenever possible, I have aimed for primary sources that are not penned by white, straight, cisgender men like me.

Privilege in the parenting space, to me, encompasses not only money but time, although in many instances money buys time for parents. When I sit in the waiting room of my children's gymnastics class reading a parenting book, I benefit from the privilege of being able to afford the book but, even more so, being able to pay for the forty-five-minute class and the brief respite from having to care for my children. This book is aimed at moms and dads who seem unable to find effective answers to quell their parenting anxieties, no matter how much they read, and acknowledges these parents will remain anxious because they cannot be perfect. I am one of these parents, but not all parents have the time and money to pose the questions, dissect the anxieties, and fret about the imperfections discussed in this book. The author and the reader are approaching this material from similar positions—curiosity, frustration, anxiety, *and* privilege.

The title I eventually used instead of *Parent—Long Days, Short Years*—draws from the expression, "The days are long, but the years are short." I've heard this phrase thrown around so much that I assumed it was an age-old maxim. I was wrong, as I often was in the process of writing this book. Gretchen Rubin, writing about her own children growing up too fast, was the first to say this (at least in print) in her 2009 book, *The Happiness Project.*[6] The sentiment, however, is as old as the Bible, with 2 Peter 3:8 reminding us that "with the Lord a day is like a thousand years, and a thousand years are like a day."

"The days are long, but the years are short" is intended primarily as a warning for parents. Enjoy your children now, even though the process of raising them can be enormously difficult, because before you know it, they will no longer be children. It's a nice sentiment, but I personally take much more solace in the advice dished out by Ada Calhoun in her recent book, *Why We Can't Sleep*: "Older people tend to be happier, and someday we will be those people."[7] The short years may not be a punishment but rather a reward for enduring all the long days of parenting. If you're at least open to this possible interpretation, I believe this is the right book for you.

1
How *Parent* Became My Verb

In June 2018, the *New Yorker*'s website posted Atul Gawande's commencement address at UCLA medical school.[1] In his speech, Gawande recalls being summoned, as a surgery resident, to see a prisoner who'd swallowed a razor blade and slashed his wrist with the corner of a toothpaste tube. As a young Gawande sutured together the strips of skin on this patient's forearm, the angry prisoner let forth a stream of abusive shouts about the hospital and its staff, the policemen guarding him, and even the amateurish suturing job Gawande was doing at that moment. "I had the urge to tell him to shut up and be a little appreciative," the now world-renowned surgeon and author told the graduating medical students. "I thought about abandoning him."

The commencement speech went viral because Gawande goes on to discuss a doctor's responsibility to all patients, both the easy and the difficult ones (or, as he calls them, the "people who are troublesome in every way: the complainer, the person with the unfriendly tone, the unwitting bigot, the guy who, as they say, makes 'poor life choices'"). When Gawande says, "The foundational principle of medicine, going back centuries, is that all lives are of equal worth," he immediately follows with, "Insisting that people are equally worthy of respect is an especially challenging idea today." He thus frames his commencement speech and his not-so-novel message of nonjudgmental doctoring in the context of 2018 and its hostile political environment. A caring, empathic physician—the kind of doctor every UCLA medical school graduate should yearn to be, the kind of doctor every patient desires—opens himself or herself to others' lives and perspectives, "to people as well as to circumstances you do not and perhaps will not understand. This is part of what I love most about this profession. It aims to sustain bedrock values that matter across all of society." In other words, doctors should model an open-minded, humanistic approach to conflict that the rest of society can follow. The speech emerged more as a Trump-era call for civility than advice for young physicians.

I, however, focused on something toward the end of Gawande's speech, when he relays to the graduates a lesson a neuroscience professor had taught his own medical school class about brain function. "When people speak, they aren't just expressing their ideas; they are, even more, expressing their emotions. And it's the emotions that they really want heard." Gawande brings this lesson back to the prisoner whose arm he was suturing.

He stopped listening to the patient's words and instead tried to listen for his emotions:

> "You seem really angry and like you feel disrespected," I said.
> "Yes," he said. "I am. I am angry and disrespected."
> His voice changed. He told me that I have no idea what it was like inside. He'd been in solitary for two years straight. His eyes began to water. He calmed down.

This exchange struck me as an obvious use of parenting language. A few months earlier, at the prompting of my wife, Xenia, I met with a parenting coach who urged me to focus on "empathy rather than solutions." Nearly every parenting book I'd read since that coaching session echoed some version of this advice. The parent's first task is to empathize with the child. Children need to know their parents recognize their emotions, so parents are encouraged to say things like "You seem sad" or "Wow, that's scary" or "I can see that you're really angry right now" when things aren't going well with their children.

Once the child feels their emotions have been validated, then that child is open to problem-solving. "Let's make a list of all the things you'd rather be doing right now than cleaning up your room," a parent might say after acknowledging that such a task does seem hard or boring or a waste of time. "And then let's quickly clean up your room together and do one or two fun things from that list." These kinds of dialogues and verbal tricks may sound forced and inauthentic, but they work. I'd been trying them more and more with my children, to the point where they'd started to come naturally, to the point where I read the Atul Gawande commencement speech and immediately compared a verbally abusive prisoner to my three-year-old son.

The challenge of medicine lies in dealing with difficult patients, and the same goes for parenting. Anyone can change a baby's poopy diaper and coo into their precious face. Struggling through a two-hour bedtime ritual, as I had been doing with Mateo, my three-year old, is an entirely different beast. Beth Ann Fennelly, in her memoir *Heating & Cooling*, wrote, "If you collected all the drops of days I've spent singing 'Row, row, row your boat' to children fighting sleep, you'd have an ocean deep enough to drown them many times over."[2] I took a picture of that sentence and returned to it often, just to remind myself that parenting is hard and frustrating and can incite faux-murderous impulses. I could have swapped Fennelly's musings for the lyrics of "Rock-a-Bye Baby" and achieved the same effect, cradle and all.

The night Mateo threw a Chapstick at my head was a turning point. He and I had been locked in a power struggle for close to an hour. He refused to stay in bed, finding one excuse after another to leave his room. He needed water. He had to pee. His butt itched. And, finally, he forgot to apply lip balm. Xenia had heard me threaten him—"If you don't go back to bed right now,

I'm going to take that Chapstick and throw it out the window"—and was approaching us when Mateo flung the lip balm at my head. She suggested I take a walk. An hour later, when I returned home to a quiet house, I confessed to her, "I get so angry that sometimes I want to scream in his face or throw the lip balm right back at him." I laughed nervously. It was hard to acknowledge how upset Mateo's behavior made me.

Xenia, who's also a physician, glared at me before replying. "God forbid you treated your patients the way you treat your kids." I'll never forgot those words, because she was right. I was a better doctor than a father. The efforts I'd put in since my first day of medical school toward being a compassionate, patient-friendly physician should have translated into my being a similarly compassionate, child-friendly parent, or at least a father who didn't fantasize about throwing lip balm at his son, but that wasn't the case. I knew it, and so did Xenia.

Some doctors are naturally endowed with excellent bedside presence. I wasn't one of them. Years ago, a patient told me, "Everything you say is important to me." He was in his late sixties and, originally from Poland, spoke English in choppy sentences that were so loud they verged upon shouts. I'd just told him that his labs were good. His newly transplanted kidney was functioning well. "I remember, I used to wake up in the night and cry," he roared, "because you said the kidney wasn't working." He started to laugh. "You said, 'Kidney no good,' and I woke up at night and cried. Isn't that funny? I was crying about my kidney." He was still laughing, and I felt obliged to return the laugh.

But I've also felt obliged to work toward improving my dialogue with patients, being more thoughtful and deliberate in my communication, always mindful that a patient should leave clinic feeling better than when they arrived, even if the overall prognosis isn't rosy. That kind of work, that effort to connect with patients on their level, had become the focus for my daily clinical practice.

With Xenia's encouragement, and with guidance from a slew of parenting resources (counselors, group sessions, magazine articles, and book after book after book), I set out to improve my parenting in the same manner I'd honed my craft as a physician. I'd learned to doctor, and now I needed to learn to parent.

When Juno was a year and half, Xenia and I took her to the New York Botanical Garden and noticed a black dot on her eyelid when we returned home. She fought us off as we tried to examine her, but eventually we were able to hold her down long enough to shine a light on her and see that that the black dot was crawling on the inside of her eyelid. I had to hold Juno down, in full restraint while she screamed and kicked and tried to bite me, while Xenia used her fingernails to pull off the tick. The whole process took over thirty minutes, and when we were done, we were all in tears. We finally calmed

Juno down with a bowl of raspberries, and then we calmed ourselves down that night with a bottle of wine. That struggle seemed like the worst thing we would ever go through, but in retrospect it was such an easy task. We had only one small child, we knew exactly what to do, and we outnumbered her two to one.

Now the kids outnumbered us and provided a never-ending supply of minor but constant crises. Mateo's biting again, Juno's refusing to practice violin, Joaquin has a diaper rash, all the kids need to be picked up before 5:00 p.m. tomorrow, we're running low on milk and have zero eggs, the basement smells moldy, our cable bill just increased by $25 a month, the cleaning lady found mouse droppings in the downstairs bathroom. "I don't want to be in a house that's so chaotic," Xenia said that night Mateo threw his Chapstick at my head. "I grew up in that kind of house. It's awful. It's bad for the kids. It was bad for me."

Being a parent, like being a doctor, was supposed to be a noble calling. I'd already come to terms with the truth that I wasn't born to be a doctor and needed to consciously employ strategies with my patients to get them better. My struggles with Mateo forced me to acknowledge that fatherhood, like medicine, wasn't my noble calling. By the time I read Atul Gawande's commencement speech online, I'd put in months of work improving my parenting. I'd read thousands of pages, attended coaching sessions, participated in parenting groups, listened to weekly podcasts, and held almost nightly recap sessions with Xenia on what was working and what wasn't. I became consumed with parenting as a task, as a skill, as something that could be mastered.

Parent had ceased being a noun and had become a verb in my life. And this pervasive verb consumed my thoughts. The rest of the world could read about Atul Gawande's experience with a difficult patient and dream about a post-Trump world in which we all listened to each other's feelings. All I wanted to do was be home with my kids and continue attuning to their needs.

2
How *Parent* Became Everyone's Verb

In addition to being a legendary pediatrician, my father was also a renowned medical educator. Splitting his time between private practice and an academic appointment, he trained, over the span of five decades, thousands of medical students and pediatric residents. During this time, he garnered so many teacher of the year awards that he ran out of space in his office to hang them all. Plaques and certificates sit stacked on the bookshelves in the guest room of my parents' house, proclaiming his teaching excellence to a room that remains empty most of the year.

"The secret to being a good attending," my dad once told me, "is letting the medical students and residents think they're doing everything on their own, when in fact you're watching everything they do. Behind the scenes, you may actually have to do a lot to ensure the patients are getting optimal care. But you want the students and house staff to think they did everything themselves."

It would make sense for my father and me to have had this conversation when I'd finally finished my own training and taken my first job as an attending physician at an academic hospital. But when I picture him sharing this secret with me—which, I recognize now, is not his unique secret but the mark of good teachers everywhere, in every field—I recall the exchange occurring much earlier in my career, when I was a medical student. He told me his teaching philosophy after I'd praised one of my own attendings, a junior faculty member who had distinguished herself by spending so much time with me and my fellow students. Unlike the more seasoned faculty, she accompanied us when we saw patients, sat beside us at the computers as we scanned labs and x-rays, and participated in all our tedious meetings with social workers and care coordinators. My father's not-so-subtle criticism of this young attending wasn't out of jealousy. Even then, he was in teaching mode, recognizing that someday I'd be in her shoes, fresh out of training and thrust into the role of attending. He wanted me to know that being omnipresent didn't necessarily translate into good mentorship.

Or so I interpreted his advice at the time. I wonder now, however, if he was also—in his own, weird, medicine-obsessed way—defending not only his teaching style, which did not need any defense given all the awards cluttering up his bookshelves, but also his parenting approach, for which he'd received no plaques from me or my brothers. Perhaps he didn't need plaques to feel justified as a father: his oldest son was a screenwriter whose first movie starred Robert De Niro, his next two sons were an orthopedic surgeon and a doctor-to-be, and his youngest son was finishing up a music degree at Haverford. His kids were successful *and* independent, and he may have felt that his hands-off approach to parenting was as important an ingredient to their accomplishments as my mom's hands-on style.

If, in fact, my father was imparting not just teaching but also parenting advice, I've ignored the latter. I let my medical students and residents experience a great deal of autonomy, or at least feel they are experiencing this freedom while I surreptitiously double-check their work. With my patients, too, I've crafted a persona of a doctor who cares about them but also has clear boundaries. I insist that all of my patients have primary care providers to handle their non-kidney issues and, because so many of these patients are seeing me as a second or third opinion consult, recommend they retain their local nephrologist for the day-to-day management of their kidney issues. I introduce patients to the fellows and junior faculty who might be answering their urgent calls on nights and weekends or when I'm traveling. I am no concierge physician, I tell my patients with these policies. You will have access to me on my terms, not yours.

But I am a concierge parent, and I've become one intentionally and with great pride. I love my father and appreciate everything he's done for me, but as soon as Juno was born, I made a deliberate effort to follow my mother's parenting model and not his. I envisioned being ever-present throughout Juno's childhood and even flirted with leaving academic medicine for a pharmaceutical industry job in which I'd never have to work weekends and could even work a day or two from home, beside my new baby. Although this parenting zeal eventually wavered, I still have remained present for my children in all of their daily doings—helping them get dressed, wiping their butts, packing their lunches, dropping them off at school, sorting through e-mails about parent-teacher conferences and school fundraisers and supplies needed for the classroom, rushing home to eat an early dinner with them, reading bedtime stories, practicing violin, searching the house for missing lovies and favorite blankets, responding to middle-of-the-night bed-wetting accidents or requests for water—in a way that my father never was for me and my brothers. As soon as I hear one of them call out for me—"Daddy! Daddy! I need you!"—I drop whatever I'm doing and race to their room. At their service.

I savor being the parent the children want and recognize how different this situation is from my father's experience. He'd come home from work late at night, often after we'd finished dinner, give us all hugs and kisses, and then head into his bedroom, where, if we wanted to, we could find him in his underwear and undershirt, lying on top of his bedsheets, poring over a medical journal. If I came in to ask him a question about homework or tell him about something sports-related or simply just to say hi, he'd put the journal down, engage with me, and even invite me to sit on the bed beside him. But these encounters were rare and, when they did occur, quite brief. I don't remember ever taking him up on the invitation to sit on the bed beside him, although I'm sure I did. I think I sensed then, as I recognize clearly now, that if he wanted to help with homework or hear about the Mets game, he wouldn't be holed up in his room clad only in his underwear.

In my father's defense, some of what I now decry as absentee parenting was pretty standard behavior at the time for someone working an incredibly stressful job with long hours and few weekends off and a wife who stayed home to raise the kids. He expected my mom to do all the parenting; his role was to provide the substrate she needed to do that. And I'm sure my father, when he played catch with us or took us to the driving range or assistant-coached one of our teams, probably reflected on how much more he was doing for his sons than *his* father, my grandfather, had done for him and his sister. I dedicated my book, *Doctor*, to my father, and my brother, Mark, called it a "love letter to Dad" when he finished reading it. He also predicted that my mother would be offended by how little she appeared in the book.

Yet I had dedicated something far bigger than a book to my mother. I had dedicated my most important assignment—being a father—to her as I tried to emulate her style of parenting. Unfortunately, I was slow to realize that I couldn't do it as well as she had. All the aspects of parenting that I'd started to see as toxic, like the performance art of holiday card poses, the humble and not-so-humble brags behind every Facebook post, the hyper-scheduling of extracurricular activities, the obsessive attention to what my kids ate and read and heard and watched and said, these were the kinds of things my mom did and excelled at in the 1970s and 1980s with me and my brothers, albeit in a more analog than digital fashion. My mom, whose first child was born in 1971, was "parenting" just when the noun had transformed into a verb but well before this verb came to represent, to quote the writer Chimamanda Ngozi Adichie, an "endless, anxious journey of guilt."[1]

Over just a few decades, parents have increased the amount of time, attention, and money applied to raising children. A mother today who works outside the home spends a similar amount of time and considerably more money (inflation-adjusted) tending her children than a stay-at-home mom did in the 1970s.[2] The usage graphs for the verb form of "parent" on Google Books Ngram Viewer (figure 2.1) could stand in for similar plots depicting hours per day or dollars per child spent by parents over the last five decades.[3]

The verb form of "parent"—in particular, its gerund "parenting"—was first employed in the United States in the late 1950s according to *The Merriam-Webster Dictionary*. However, Fitzhugh Dodson's 1970 book, *How to Parent*, is credited with introducing the verb to a wide

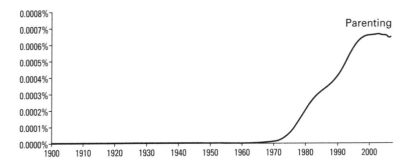

Figure 2.1

The Google Books Ngram Viewer charts the frequencies of any set of search strings using a yearly count of n-grams found in sources printed since 1500 in Google's text corpora in English, Chinese, French, German, Hebrew, Italian, Russian, and Spanish. The x-axis denotes the year in which works were published; the y-axis shows the frequency with which the n-gram appears throughout the corpus. This usage graph plots the abrupt rise of "parenting" in works published between 1970 and 2000.

audience, defined as "to use with tender loving care all the information science has accumulated about child psychology in order to raise happy and intelligent human beings."[4] The book became an international best seller and, in turn, irrevocably transformed parenthood from someone *to be* into something *to do*. Modern parents, who've had fifty years since the book's publication to absorb the aforementioned "endless, anxious journey of guilt," would likely be shocked reading *How to Parent* today. Dodson repeatedly advocates spanking and compares disciplining children to training and domesticating animals. These harsh precepts were advanced during a time, as Jennifer Senior points out in

All Joy and No Fun, when "women were yanking off their aprons, taking the Pill, and fighting for the Equal Rights Amendment."[5]

The verb form of "parent" entered common usage not because of Dodson's particular parenting advice but because his book and verb promised empowerment, particularly to women who were leaving home for the workforce in increasing numbers. Raising children was now repurposed as a skill or science that could be learned, practiced, and eventually mastered. This transformation wasn't limited solely to working mothers either. Around this time, the nomenclature for non-working mothers shifted from "housewife" to "stay-at-home mom." Senior elucidates why this not-so-minor change in title reflected an overall new cultural emphasis: "The pressures on women [had] gone from keeping an immaculate *house* to being an irreproachable *mom*."

Pressure, as Senior uses the word, is a euphemism for anxiety, which has been a driving force behind shifts in American parenting styles since the country's inception.[6] A theme emerges when exploring parental anxieties from generation to generation: parents have always focused their concerns on what they can try to control rather than what they know they cannot. Indeed, the awareness that so many crucial factors in a child's development are beyond a parent's control often fuels a parent's anxiety about what is seemingly controllable. *This is one area I can make a difference, so I better not mess it up*. If we view the seventeenth-century Pilgrims and

Puritans as the earliest American parents (recognizing, of course, the thousands of Indigenous parents already here at the time), we already see the pattern in place. The Puritans should have feared infection, the most likely cause of death for everyone in the family, but instead aimed their parenting efforts at rooting out corruption and sin in their children.[7]

Three hundred years later, post-war parents were powerless against the threat of nuclear attack but could control whether their children ate enough servings of fruits, vegetables, bread, and dairy each day. Parents in the 1970s and 1980s seem, from today's vantage point, irrationally obsessed with a fear of kidnapping, which may reflect a more deep-seated worry about whether the entry of women into the workforce was a form of child abandonment. The tendency for parents today to control their children's time via over-scheduling of "enrichment" activities could be interpreted as a response (rational or irrational) to concerns about child safety, especially in light of the potential dangers lurking on nearby screens. The more likely drive toward the "concerted cultivation" of children, however, is a fear response to economic anxieties. The current generation of parents is the first to have less overall wealth, on average, than the preceding generation of parents. This trend is expected to continue, not reverse. And with rare exceptions, parents today are no longer training their children for a skilled trade or a place in the family business. The overscheduling of the middle-class child with violin lessons and Chinese language tutors and indoor soccer leagues may feel like, as Nora Ephron joked, "force-feeding it like a foie gras goose."[8] In truth, the (Ephron's words again) "altering, modifying, modulating, manipulating, smoothing out, improving" efforts that embody twenty-first-century parenting are a fear-driven attempt to prepare children for the harsh economic landscape awaiting them at the end of childhood.

Anxiety alone does not explain the immersive, all-in approach to raising children that has made parenting a competitive and often unenjoyable sport. The demographics have changed too. Parents today are older when they first take on the role of mom or dad (the average age at first birth for college-educated women now exceeds thirty years of age) compared to their own parents and grandparents. And with older age comes fewer children, so that today's kids can consume greater and greater quantities of their parents' attention. I had three brothers and am hard-pressed to remember classmates who were only children; the few I can remember were the children of divorce, and most had half-siblings (and entirely separate families) against whom they were competing for their parents' time.

Postponing parenthood also gives couples more years of childless freedom against which their child-rearing years can be compared. The before versus after contrast can be taxing on parents who may question why they relinquished this freedom to join the ranks of a stressed, exhausted, and often miserable cohort. Non-parents consistently report being happier, when quantified in studies, than parents.[9] Interestingly, the country with the greatest gap in happiness levels between parents and non-parents is the United States, by a significant margin (the differences in such levels correlate, to some degree, with the availability of childcare and other nationally provided welfare benefits). Parental unhappiness may not be a new phenomenon, but open discussion about such unhappiness clearly has hit its stride in the modern era. Unhappy parents who believe that "better" children hold the key to unlocking a secret realm of family happiness are willing to try (and buy) anything to reach that goal.

Finally, the rising age of moms and dads produces more space between their childhood and parenthood to reflect on what their own parents did, right and wrong. Many moms and dads actively parent, with all that verb's connotations, to contrast directly with how their parents handled the same responsibilities. Children today claim their parents' attention twenty-four hours a day, seven days a week. The normalization of such claims by modern parenting can be seen as a direct response to the prior generation's hands-off and, at times, neglectful style of parenting. Again, this is not a new phenomenon. In her sweeping history of child-rearing in the United States, *The End of American Childhood*, historian Paula Fass lays out how each subsequent era in this country (her divisions are roughly every fifty years) has slowly chipped away at the "belief in the sturdy independence of children that was a fact of life in the early nineteenth century."[10]

The pushback against earlier parents' mores is not new, but the degree and accelerated pace of the pushback is a modern phenomenon. As mentioned above, I know my father, like most men of his generation, considered his involvement with me and my brothers as a significant improvement over the scant time and attention he received from my grandfather. Still, my father's parenting efforts were only slightly improved compared to my grandfather's. And these slightly improved efforts would be considered laughable in contrast to what modern dads regularly do (e.g., my brothers and I have never eaten any food—meal or snack—prepared by my father).

The pressures on today's mothers to outdo their own moms is even greater, incorporating both internal and external (i.e., society-driven) expectations. In *Why We Can't Sleep: Women's New Midlife Crisis*, Ada Calhoun states that Generation X mothers—loosely defined as moms who were born between the years 1965 and 1980—are infected with "a particularly virulent strain" of the "having-it-all" virus. Today's moms grew up in an era when women, for the first time, were actively encouraged to do more and be better than men. The encouragement was not always overt, of course, but the messages were clear as women entered the workforce in increasing numbers. Commercials from the 1970s and 1980s showed working moms entering their immaculate homes with hair perfectly styled and makeup freshly applied. These wide-eyed moms practically danced their way into the kitchen, pirouetted into an apron, and prepared gourmet meals for their deliriously happy and appreciative husbands and kids. The actual working moms from this era didn't have time to watch such commercials, but their daughters did as part of what Calhoun calls "an experiment in crafting a higher-achieving, more fulfilled, more well-rounded version of the American woman."[11]

The message didn't just come from commercials. Moms raising their Generation X daughters often made a point of telling these girls how "lucky" they were to be growing up at a time when they could study any subject, take any job, live anywhere, *and* still raise a family. These exhortations were not meant to be burdensome or shaming. In an era when working outside the home was deemed the clearest expression of female empowerment, mothers felt the need to cast their child-rearing responsibilities as another, equally important expression of women's power. Such power only grew the better a woman performed such responsibilities, the more facile she was at the newly popular verb form of parenting. In a relatively short period of time, however, performance guilt and frustrations about not "having-it-all" began to chip away at the possibility of child-rearing as a statement of female empowerment.

If I had followed my father's example as a parent, rather than as a doctor, I should have taken a step back from my kids. I should have created more space, less hovering, more independence, less reliance. I should have hired more help. I should have carved out more time to exercise or read or run errands without any children beside me. I should have taken care of myself as much as I was taking care of the children. I found a few texts that advocated such an approach, articles and books that advanced parent advocacy over children-centric lifestyles. They made sense but still seemed wrong. And these books were not routinely reviewed in the *New York Times*, discussed on NPR, or suggested by my amazon.com purchasing algorithm.

So instead of taking a step back, I continued to plunge further and further ahead, beyond child-rearing books and into parenting seminars, where I took notes and regurgitated them back to a group of equally anxious parents. I lay on the floor beside Mateo's bed while we listened to guided meditation videos for children on YouTube, soundtracks that only helped me fall asleep. I continued to post pictures of my kids on Facebook, but now each one communicated a subtext of how hard I was trying to be a good father. Here's Mateo filling out the breakfast menu I made for him, so that we no longer have to argue about what he wants to eat each morning. Here's Juno reading Joaquin a Sandra Boynton book in Spanish, because Xenia and I are doing such an amazing job raising our kids bilingually. Here are Juno and Mateo shoveling snow from the driveway while singing a Car Seat Headrest song, because my kids are cooperative enough to do chores, and cool enough to pick up on all the wonderful music to which I'm exposing them. In other words, I kept asking myself the question, "Why am I good doctor but a bad father?" And I pushed on and on, assuming that I'd eventually find an answer. Like most parents I know.

3
Playing the Role of Parent

In 1979, Adele Faber and Elaine Mazlish published *How to Talk So Kids Will Listen & Listen So Kids Will Talk.*[1] Roughly four decades later, in 2017, Faber's daughter Joanna (with her own coauthor, Julie King) published *How to Talk So Little Kids Will Listen.*[2] The symmetry is cute if you can stomach the obvious nepotism of the publishing industry. A scan of the titles, however, and a closer examination of the books themselves reveal a significant discrepancy between these seemingly parallel best sellers. Adele Faber and Elaine Mazlish wrote about talking *and* listening to children. Joanna Faber and Julie King have streamlined their suggestions to just talking.

The differences in these titles and their contents can potentially be explained by changes in publishing trends. In 2017, consumers wanted shorter books and, presumably, shorter titles. Plus, the name recognition of the Faber brand didn't require a full, somewhat bulky title of *How to Talk So Little Kids Will Listen & Listen So Little Kids Will Talk.* Just like Dunkin' Donuts would drop "Donuts" from its brand without losing any of its

popularity, so too could the *How to Talk* series thrive
with an abbreviated moniker. Beyond marketing and
sales, however, lies the argument that the listening component of the original *How to Talk So Kids Will Listen &
Listen So Kids Will Talk* had become accepted dogma by
2017. In 1979, parents could read with fresh eyes about
the importance of listening for emotional cues in their
children's speech. A child's need for their feelings to be
heard and acknowledged seems intuitive today, in large
part due to the parenting footprint left behind by Faber
and Mazlish's book. Today, any mother or father reaching for a parenting book presumably already knows the
importance of empathy and just needs to know how to
wield this empathy in the most effective manner.

Both Adele Faber and Elaine Mazlish trained in the-
ater before becoming parenting experts. And this the-
atrical background, I believe, provides the primary
explanation for why the twenty-first-century iteration of their landmark book puts all of its emphasis on
how to talk to children. In *How to Talk So Kids Will Listen & Listen So Kids Will Talk* and their next book, *Siblings without Rivalry*, Faber and Mazlish provided comic
book–like representations of parents talking to children
the right way and the wrong way. The dialogue in these
illustrated panels served as language guides—playbooks,
scripts—for parents struggling to connect with their
children. There is a clear progression in the authors'
work toward more comics and less straightforward text.
By the time their following book appeared, the comics

had taken on essentially equal weight to the theory and advice that introduced these scenarios. Not surprisingly, this next book bears no mention of listening in its title: *How to Talk So Kids Can Learn—At Home and in School.*

Joanna Faber and Julie King use comics in their 2017 book in this same way, as the reward for parents who have made their way through the preceding chapters' texts on cooperation, praise, tattling, and shyness (to name just a few of their book's topics). The reward lies in seeing how the theory can be applied in practice, but the reward also comes in the form of an actual script that parents can use when trying to talk to their children. Faber and King recommend that parents rip out pages from their book, if necessary, and keep them in purses or glove compartments, taped to refrigerators or bathroom mirrors, stuffed into back pockets or backpacks, as constant reminders of how to get their lines right. They treat parents like actors in a play who need help learning their lines.

The parenting advice industry has been around, as Jennifer Traig half-jokes, since "the time the second human couple got pregnant and the first one realized there were now people who knew less about raising children than they did."[3] In America, the end of the nineteenth century saw two major shifts that transformed parenting advice. The first was the move of more and more families into rapidly growing cities, a migration that put moms and dads farther away from their own parents than previous generations. The second was the significant reduction in infant mortality due to improvements in hygiene. With survival no longer as pressing a concern, parents now felt compelled to focus on how best to *raise* their children. And with grandma and grandpa now tens or hundreds of miles away, these parents needed new sources for child-rearing advice and increasingly turned to printed texts.[4]

The earliest parenting books blended practical, usually hygiene-focused recommendations with a smattering of philosophical principles aimed toward raising respectful and ultimately independent children: a teaspoon of cod liver oil with each meal right alongside warnings about sparing the rod and spoiling the child. Over time, though, parenting books dropped the former and focused entirely on the latter, exemplified by the works of Louis Starr, who had a hit in the 1890s with *Hygiene of the Nursery*[5] and approximately twenty years later was penning books like *The Adolescent Period: Its Features and Management.*[6] This shift in focus away from "hygiene" and toward "management" required—at least if an author wanted to sell books—softer language and a healthy dose of reassurance for anxious parents.

The bible of this softer, parent-friendly approach was Benjamin Spock's *The Common Sense Book of Baby and Child Care.*[7] Comparing Dr. Spock's book, which has sold over fifty million copies since its 1946 publication, to the Bible is appropriate. First, for many years only the actual

Bible outsold Spock's book. Then parenting classes using the book as a guide for weekly discussions, akin to a regular Bible study meeting, sprang up across the country. And *The Common Sense Book of Baby and Child Care*, both in real life and in popular culture, found a footing as the definitive, bedside reference for moms and dads (recall the leitmotif of an increasingly tattered, paperback copy of Spock's book bouncing around from scene to scene, along with the kidnapped infant, in the Coen brothers' film *Raising Arizona*). Spock opened his book with the now-famous mantra, "Trust yourself. You know more than you think you do," which is the parenting version of "In the beginning, God created the heaven and the earth."

Spock's advice for parents was far from revolutionary. The success of his book was predicated entirely on relaying a message that parents of the nascent baby boom were eager to hear: Don't stress about schedules. Feed your children when they're hungry and put them to bed when they're tired. Pick them up if they cry, and leave them alone when they seem content. Hug and kiss them as much as you like. Overall, Spock urged his parental readers, trust your instincts! Five years before *The Common Sense Book of Baby and Child Care*, an article in *Parents' Magazine* expressed concern that one of the unintended consequences of the growing fields of child study and child-rearing advice was a novel form of parental anxiety. "Relax and enjoy your children," the magazine exhorted its readers.[8] Spock expanded this tagline to a book-length version.

I worked with a public speaking coach during my last year of fellowship training. I'd been invited to give a talk at a national meeting, and my division chief worried that my lecturing skills would not reflect well on his program. The speaking coach sat through a practice run of my talk and had two simple suggestions: first, remove half the slides, and second, memorize the talk. "Simplify your message," she said, "so that it comes across undiluted. And have the talk so committed to memory that you could give it without looking at the slides, as if you're reciting lines from a script. That will take away most, if not all, of your nerves." Her suggestions worked, not just for that talk but for every subsequent lecture I've given since that session, and I've passed along those two recommendations to colleagues and trainees who've shared their own angst about public speaking.

What I haven't passed along, until now, is something else that speaking coach said to me during our first session. After watching my practice lecture, and before giving me the two useful suggestions mentioned above, she asked me to name a "good" public speaker, someone I wished I could sound like when I was at the podium. "Barack Obama," I answered. "He *is* a wonderful speaker, isn't he?" she asked. "It seems like he was born with a gift to speak in public, doesn't it?" I nodded yes to her questions. "He was," she then said, "and you weren't. So you'll need to work on this."

In their book *Now Say This: The Right Words to Solve Every Parenting Dilemma*, family therapists Heather Turgeon and Julie Wright advocate an approach to parenting that parallels the public speaking coach's advice on lecturing.[9] They've simplified their message to a handy acronym, ALP, which stands for attune, limit set, and problem solve. And they provide a set of scripts incorporating the ALP method that parents can memorize and recite verbatim to their children. The ALP strategy is not particularly unique. Many parenting books, including the aforementioned *How to Talk . . .* books, promote a similar approach to the child-in-crisis. Start with empathy, then introduce reality, and together come up with a creative solution. The scripts in *Now Say This*, therefore, strike conventional notes: "You don't want to leave the park now because you're having so much fun," one such script begins. "But it's starting to get dark and we need to go home for dinner. Do you want to skip to the car or have me carry you on my shoulders?" *Now Say This* emerges as a singular title, a parenting book I never thought I'd encounter, in its explicit instructions to parents that these scripts can and should be memorized. The *How to Talk . . .* books hinted at this approach but never took the final leap to where *Now Say This* was bold enough to go.

Turgeon and Wright established their credentials as parenting experts—and, in some households, divine saviors—with their first book, *The Happy Sleeper*.[10]

Children, from birth, have an innate biological ability and a strong physiologic need to sleep well, they argued in this best seller. Most sleep issues lie at the feet of the parents and not the kids. Specifically, parents are too anxious, hovering, and present when their children are trying to sleep. With their Sleep Wave technique, which essentially translates to putting the baby down while awake and employing regimented five-minute checks only if the baby is crying, they introduced the concept of scripts with a three-sentence mantra to be uttered during the five-minute checks. "Mommy (or Daddy) is here. I love you. Night, night." *The Happy Sleeper* encouraged parents to be consistent and almost machine-like in their bedtime routines. Do the same activities in the same order leading up to putting the baby down to sleep, and stick to the five-minute intervals and the three-sentence script if the baby is crying. Let us design bedtime for you, Turgeon and Wright offered in this book, and we'll get your kids to sleep all night long.

Now Say This takes this approach to bedtime and expands it to the rest of the day. Turgeon and Wright have offered up scripts for how to deal with a range of parenting struggles, from babies who pull their parents' hair to eye-rolling preteens, from siblings who fight with each other to toddlers who refuse to brush their teeth. This seems like a radical leap. It's one thing for parents to admit they can't handle bedtime, quite another thing for parents to prefer following someone else's blueprint rather than their own at all hours of the day. *Now Say*

This rests upon two assumptions—the first, that parent-hood can be scripted, and the second, that it should—and makes no apologies for these beliefs. Turgeon and Wright are calling out parents' lack of natural instincts and gifts the same way that public speaking coach did to me years ago. We are a long way from Dr. Spock reassuring parents to trust themselves. Seventy-two years after *The Common Sense Book of Baby and Child Care*, two best-selling family therapists are stressing the polar opposite in their message to parents.

The success of this thoroughly modern approach to parenting advice hinges upon a consumer group of anxious, frustrated, and exhausted parents who are more than willing to hand over control to a perceived authority. Turgeon and Wright illustrate this dynamic when they relay the genesis of *Now Say This* in its introductory chapter. During their book tour for *The Happy Sleeper*, the question and answer sessions inevitably extended beyond sleep issues to general parenting concerns. As Turgeon or Wright relayed an answer to a parent's question, employing some version of an ALP script (before they'd formally named the approach), the mothers and fathers in the audience frantically scribbled down their responses. After the talks, these same parents approached the authors and showed them their notes to make sure they got the words exactly right.

Kim Brooks begins her book, *Small Animals: Parent-hood in the Age of Fear*, with the story of how she left her four-year-old son in the parking lot of a strip mall while she ran inside, for five minutes, to buy him a replacement pair of headphones.[11] While she was in the store, someone called the police to report what he or she deemed delinquent behavior. In trying to understand why a stranger would feel compelled to do such a thing, Brooks realizes that she had "tapped into a common and long-established tradition of mother-shaming, the communal ritual of holding up a woman as a 'bad mother,' a symbol on which we can unleash our collective, mother-related anxieties, insecurities, and rage." Her book explores why parenting and fear have become synonymous, concluding that "the object of fear correlates less to the level of risk than to parents' ability (or perceived ability) to exert control over the outcome." Parents dissect and analyze their every action, their every word, their every gesture and endow them with far-reaching implications for their children's long-term futures. Is it any surprise, then, that such anxious parents are more than willing to recite a family therapist–penned script rather than improvise their own lines?

My brother told me recently that he was having some behavioral issues with his two-year-old, and when I pressed *Now Say This* onto him, explaining its modus operandi, he brayed at the idea of reciting prefab lines to his crying son. Because my brother is an executive, I appealed to his work life. "If you had to have an uncomfortable conversation with an employee," I said, "like if you had to fire someone, wouldn't you plan out what you were going to say beforehand, and try to have that conversation go as close to your plan as possible?" He would, he conceded, and eventually said he'd read the book, although I doubt he will. Not yet. He didn't seem anxious enough. He still thought that he and his wife, on their own, could right the ship. He had yet to realize what Kim Brooks calls "our darkest fear as parents: the fear of failure."

I had long ago conceded that I'd realized such fear when I saw the black eye my seven-year-old daughter gave my four-year-old son "by accident," or when I watched my one-year-old mimic their shouting at the dinner table, and perhaps that is why I was so willing to follow the scripts penned by Turgeon and Wright. Why I snapped photos of the book for my phone's camera roll and snuck peeks for suggested lines before knocking on Juno's locked bedroom door ("What are you trying to communicate to me right now?") or responding to Mateo's repeated requests for a snack ("It's almost dinnertime, and it's important to keep your belly empty so that you'll enjoy the meal"). In *Small Animals*, Kim Brooks compares her irrational fears as a parent to her childhood terrors of a wolf that lived in the back of her closet.

> The wolf was going to eat me, though I begged him
> not to. He could not be reasoned with. He could not
> be appeased. The wolf was clever and well-spoken,
> and one day, amused by my pleading, he told me that
> if I counted to fifty before I fell asleep every night, he

would stay in the closet; he would not come out. I still remember how I lay in bed, tight beneath the covers, counting slowly in my head. It made no sense, but I believed it. I knew that if I counted, I'd be safe. One, two, three, four, I counted every night, all the way to fifty. I never doubted or wavered in my counting. I wanted to be safe.

So many parents want that safety too, and, like the little girl that Brooks once was, seek solace in words.

In addition to scripts for parents to recite to their children, Turgeon and Wright in *Now Say This* also provide mantras for parents to say to themselves in their worst moments, when they must seclude themselves from their children for a few seconds to calm down and muster up the strength to reenter the fray of modern parenting. "I can handle this" is one such mantra. It may not be true, but it's simple, and it's easy to memorize. If anxious parents rehearse their lines enough, they can deliver the performance their kids need.

"Why do I need these things?" my patient asked angrily at the beginning of her appointment. "Do you know how many side effects these pills have?" She ruffled through her purse and produced the drug's package insert, which unfolded took up the space of a large map. She pointed her finger at the section detailing the medicine's adverse effects. Did she think I was unaware of the drug's potential toxicities? Did she believe she had uncovered some secret about this medication that would change my mind? I'd published dozens of articles and lectured around the world on her specific kidney disease. "This is crazy," she continued, pounding the desk with her finger as she pointed to the list of side effects. "My body can't handle this right now. You're going to have to prescribe something else." She grabbed the package insert off the table and, not bothering to fold it back up, stuffed it into her purse.

I took a deep breath and cleared my throat. When it's important that my patients buy into everything I say, I pretend that I'm a doctor from television, taller and better-looking and more confident than the doctor I really am. I picture Don Draper from *Mad Men*, decked out in a long white coat. I love the way my voice sounds when I take on this persona. "I know you're scared and I know you're angry," I said in a Draper-esque baritone. "I also know you're a strong woman who can handle this situation." She straightened up in her chair. "I see the kind of patient who will respond to the medicine and years later will be sitting across from me, feeling great, and saying something like, 'Remember when I was so upset about everything?' And she'll be laughing and happy. That's what I see. That's why I chose this medicine—it has the best chance of working with the least chance of hurting you." I sat motionless after finishing my little speech. Silence filled the exam room for what seemed like forever but was probably only ten or fifteen seconds.

"You promise?" the patient asked. "If you promise, I'll take the pills."

"I promise I will always be working to help you. I'll always recommend what I think is in your best interest." I was still in full Dr. Don Draper mode. "You can do this."

When I was a medical student, one of my attending physicians told me that patients wanted their doctors to look and speak like the doctors on television. In part he was giving me some grooming tips (I desperately needed a shave and a haircut when he shared this advice), but he was also hinting at the idea that physicians could be living versions of placebo therapy if they so choose. When we think of placebo effects in medicine, we generally think of the sham pill or procedure that patients unwittingly consume, usually in the setting of a clinical trial. But doctors themselves can be living and breathing placebos. Natasha Campbell and Amir Raz, two placebo experts, describe how physicians "have the ability to change expectancy, experience, and outcome by capitalizing on certain conditioned social cues and choosing words wisely, in order to create an optimal healing environment."[12] Replace the word "physicians" with "parents" and eliminate the word "healing," and this last statement would fit neatly into a parenting book. When I told Mateo that I could sprinkle magic, invisible dust on his pillow to help him fall asleep faster, my intentions were not that different from when I told a patient that a high dose of vitamin D would help with some of his fatigue and chronic pain issues.

The opposite of the placebo effect is what the medical literature has dubbed the "nocebo" effect, when a doctor confirms a patient's expectation of hopelessness that a negative situation will not get better, no matter what one does to alleviate it. The invisible sleeping dust didn't work with Mateo, probably because I myself didn't completely buy into its capabilities. In fact, the dread I felt some nights, ushering him back into bed for the tenth or eleventh time, giving yet another back rub, tightly tucking in his blanket so that it might serve as a pseudo-straight jacket, knowing he'd be bouncing around his room within moments of my closing the door, all of this anxiety on my part was likely supporting a *nocebo* effect with Mateo's bedtime and his angst about falling asleep. I was finally able to get some success with Mateo's sleep routine when I convinced him that sleep was important for his health. "If you want to grow up to be as big and smart as Juno, you need to get as much sleep as possible, every night," I whispered. Because I believed those words, thankfully so did Mateo.

When parenting experts like Adele Faber and Elaine Mazlish or Heather Turgeon and Julie Wright provide scripts and dialogues for parents to follow and, in extreme cases, memorize, they are tapping into the placebo component of effective parenting. After all, probably the most commonly prescribed placebo across the world is a parent kissing a child's boo-boo better. The revolution that Faber and Mazlish began with their book in 1979, which has been carried through to modern parenting texts, is the recognition and acceptance of the performative aspects of parenting. Moms and dads don't need to enjoy all the parts of raising children, but they do need to hit their marks. I say the same thing to medical students who worry about having difficult conversations with patients. The patients will remember what you say and how you say it, so rehearse beforehand. And, if needed, pretend you're a doctor on a television or movie screen.

The night after I convinced my patient to take her medicine, I used almost the exact same script with Juno when she was throwing a fit about practicing her violin. Bach's Minuet in G Major (or Minuet 3, if you're a Suzuki family) had drained all of her self-esteem as a budding musician. In response, she was striking her bow against the floor. Don Draper wasn't a great role model as a father, but I'd just seen the Mr. Rogers documentary on Netflix, so I aped his voice and verbal mannerisms. "I promise to help you with every note, every line," I said softly. I got down on my knees and looked her in the eyes. "You can do this." And she could.

4
For Sale

Joaquin, my youngest, was rubbing at his groin. He was about two months into toilet training, and I worried that he was inspecting a newly wet spot. Our family was at a large Barnes & Noble store. His diaper bag hung on my shoulder, no longer filled with diapers and wipes but instead housing a plastic grocery bag for wet clothes and two complete sets of dry clothes. This wouldn't be our first accident outside the house. When I got down on my knees beside him, I asked him if he was wet. He shook his head no. I put the palm of my hand against his pants to check myself, and he was in fact dry. "Are you touching yourself because you want to make a pee pee?" I asked as calmly, as non-confrontationally, as supportively as possible, the way the parenting books encouraged such inquiries. He shook his head no again while tightening his grip on his pants.

I gently scooped him up into my arms and started walking toward the store's bathrooms. Joaquin whined into my ear that he didn't want to go pee pee. I promised him we could use the Disney timer in the bathroom to see how fast he could make his pee pee and get back to the children's section of the store. "We can use Kachow?" he asked. "Yes," I said. This compromise made him smile. His "Kachow" referred to Lightning McQueen from the *Cars* movies, who was one of dozens of Disney characters that encouraged my kids to brush their teeth every morning and night via my phone's Disney/Oral B timer app. Inside the bookstore's bathroom, Joaquin watched a toothbrush scrub away at a picture of Lightning McQueen and his friend, Mater, lounging at the beach. He peed and washed his hands (with water only—another concession) in just under a minute, then darted back to join his siblings in the children's section.

The bathrooms were situated by the section of the store devoted to parenting books. I scanned the new releases shelf first, then backed away to take in the nine bookshelves devoted to parenting books. The sheer number of books promising to help parents was overwhelming. As I headed back to my family, I passed by the store's cookbook section (six bookshelves), travel section (three bookshelves), science section (three bookshelves), and poetry section (one shelf). In this particular Barnes & Noble, it turned out, only children's books and adult fiction took up more real estate than parenting books.

Most parenting books focus on infants, toddlers, and preschoolers. There are plenty of volumes devoted to elementary school–aged children, and how-to-deal-with-adolescents is its own, well-represented genre. As children's dependence on their parents has spread past the high school and college years, a new category of "boomerang kids" and their own, attendant literature has emerged, too, with titles like *How to Keep Your Kid from Moving Back Home after College*[1] and *Getting to 30: A Parent's Guide to the 20-Something Years* gaining popularity among frustrated parents wondering what happened to their promised, empty nest.[2] Still, the sum of all the parenting books focused on children (and grown-up children) from kindergarten to post-schooling doesn't come close to matching the seemingly infinite volumes offering parents a guide to raising their infants, toddlers, and preschoolers.

Publishers are not experts in child psychology or developmental biology, but they know their consumer groups. Parents today are expected to spend more on their children before the age of six than at any other age in their lifetime,[3] an astounding statistic in light of college tuition rates. Consumption of parenting books only contributes a measly portion to the cost of getting a newborn to their first day of elementary school. Some of the expenditures are absolute necessities: clothes, diapers, formula, day care, car seats, strollers, and high chairs. Other expenses, however, are hard to justify as basic requirements unless you happen to exist in a bubble, which many anxious parents feel like they do, that considers any form of child deprivation abusive. Hence the multiple volumes of Baby Einstein books and matching CDs so your infant can learn songs in French, Spanish,

Chinese, and Italian. Or the Monday gymnastics class, Tuesday music lesson, Wednesday Mommy-and-Me yoga session, Thursday art class, and Friday story time at the local bookstore.

Nearly all of the commercial products geared toward parents of young children carry a subtext of improving the parenting experience. They offer more control over a child *and* the promise of a parenting stand-in, an alloparent in the form of a mass-produced good, to ensure a child's development. Consider the evolution of the baby monitor, from a makeshift walkie-talkie with a ten-foot radius to a high-tech surveillance system that can now be accessed remotely from a mobile phone anywhere in the world. "Baby monitor" is a misnomer nowadays, as these video setups are being advertised for use in infants' and toddlers' bedrooms too.

William Doherty coined the phrase "consumer parenting" to describe the style of American child-rearing in which a child lays claim to their parents' attention twenty-four hours a day, seven days a week.[4] The word "consumer" is a relevant descriptor, as much of this attention today comes in the form of purchased goods and services. Children can only feel entitled to continuous and endless devotion from their parents provided the parents are willing accomplices. The not-so-subtle transformation over the last four decades of child-rearing into a competitive sport has brought along the drive to have the best equipment for this sport. New parents are like the amateur golfer who insists on having the lightest clubs, the most comfortable cleats, the balls promising the farthest distance, the Titleist hat, the Nike shirt, and the handheld GPS device that reads out the exact distance to the pin. Stepping up to the tee, the amateur golfer is still anxious, but the gear, the getup, the proximity to professionalism make them just a little bit more confident.

In *Savage Park*, a book-length essay that examines American attitudes about play, space, and risk, Amy Fusselman researches why a baby bathtub ring she used for her two older sons is no longer on the market for her newborn daughter. In the period between her second and third child, the Consumer Federation of American had worked to ban the seats due to the risk of a drowning death should a baby topple out of the seat while their busy parents were elsewhere. Fusselman argues the problem was not the seat itself but parents' belief that these seats could protect their babies while they were gone. She lingers on a sentence from the Consumers Union (the nonprofit publisher of *Consumer Reports* magazine) in its report on these bath seats—"a parent can become distracted, and a child should not have to pay with her or his life as a result"— and asks her readers to consider what protection the now defunct bath seat product was actually selling to parents. "It is not, ultimately, the baby," Fusselman writes. "It is the parent's 'right' to become distracted."[5]

Modern parents, according to Paula Fass in *The End of American Childhood*, have reacted to their difficulties in understanding the changes that have occurred to childhood from their own memories (simple, fun, easy) to their current dilemmas (tantrums, hyper-schedules, pressure) by focusing on control. "Control, above all, became the guiding principle of 'successful' parenting during the past thirty years," Fass laments.[6] Parents have prioritized control over independence and freedom in reaction to their fears over the safety, success, and security of their children. When control is for sale, anxious parents are ready to pay no matter the cost.

By the time Joaquin "graduates" from his day care (in a full ceremony replete with tiny caps-and-gowns, a soundtracked slide show, choreographed song performances, diplomas, gift bags, and photo booths), Xenia and I will have paid close to $300,000 in day care tuition for our three children. As mentioned in chapter 2, the difference in happiness levels between parents and nonparents is largest in countries with the least generous welfare benefits (not surprisingly, the United States has consistently been the clear leader in this happiness gap). Yet the mountainous fees I've paid for childcare don't fuel my unhappiness the way watching my children hit each other or refuse to eat dinner does. In fact, I register either no response or a slight nod of approval when I receive an email notification from my bank that Joaquin's monthly tuition has been automatically paid from my checking account. The $1,695 monthly fees give him access to a preschool franchise that promises to deliver "a high-quality, play-based learning program" from 7:00 a.m. to 6:00 p.m., using "the most current, academically endorsed methods to ensure that children have fun while learning the skills they need for long-term success in school and in life."[7] Every night, Xenia and I receive an emailed report from the day care detailing that day's "lesson plan" with specifics on his journey through cognitive development, creative art, language arts, motor skills, music and movement, outside play, and yoga.

Besides the tuition fees, this all sounds too good to be true. I know. I hardly ever read the daily emails because, on the rare occasions I have, the content is boilerplate material that's indistinguishable from previous reports. Still, I buy the product of a day care with personalized lesson plans because I'd rather believe that I am paying for Joaquin's development than just finding a place to drop him off for up to eleven hours (if needed). By appealing to my desire for a sense of control, and recognizing that I am a consumer as much as a parent, the day care has locked onto the same marketing scheme that Baby Einstein, indoor playgrounds, child-centric streaming services, bilingual puzzles, learn-to-read board games, the seemingly infinite number of marker options offered by Crayola, and volume after volume of child-rearing books have mastered. Sinking parents can buy themselves lifeboats. Distressed parents can buy their way out of trouble. Concerned parents can buy themselves some relief because, with these products, they are buying a better version of parenting. Or what appears to be a better version of parenting.

Consumer parenting is big business. Sorry, I should say Big Business, as the average cost in today's America of raising a child to age seventeen approaches a quarter of a million dollars and certainly warrants capitalization. The high costs of commercialized parenting begin even prior to a child's birth, with couples encouraged to take a "babymoon" for one last relaxing, childless vacation[8] and expecting fathers urged to buy an extravagant "push present" to bestow on the mom-to-be when she emerges from labor.[9] The hyperinflated price of parenting is not just reflective of those parents who have the luxury of hiring SAT tutors, piano teachers, and swimming coaches. Low-income couples and single parents are currently spending, on average, $170,000 to $180,000 per child as well.[10] Unfortunately, some of the hardest workers in this industry receive the smallest cut of the business. Child day care workers in the United States, for example, earned a mean wage of just $12.05 per hour in 2020, averaging out to an annual wage of $25,060.[11] Over 25 percent of these workers, who are overwhelmingly women of color, live at or below the poverty line for their state.[12]

Our parental anxieties and obsessive need for control are the "why" behind such exorbitant costs, but an equally important question is the "how" behind such expenses. The majority of new parents expect they will spend more on their children than they've ever spent on themselves, but only the select few who've done some prenatal expense planning (perhaps via the assistance of a well-compensated financial planner, whose fees, like the babymoon and push gift, aren't included in the $250,000 price tag per child) have an accurate idea of these costs. Many parents start college savings funds for their newborns, gaining some solace from the idea that a small contribution today will grow, over time, into a sizable amount by the time their children reach university age. College tuition is not some well-kept secret, however.

The cumulative costs of raising a baby to school age, on the other hand, are like hidden fees that can be shocking when reviewed at the end of a billing cycle. And because prior generations spent significantly less money on their children—primarily because there were fewer products to buy—there is limited opportunity for new parents to receive spending advice from their elders the way, for example, an older neighbor wisely suggested to Xenia and me that we place a hot water bottle in Juno's crib for ten minutes before putting her down to sleep. What I wish this neighbor had suggested, in addition to the hot water bottle, was to pay for only one streaming service and never buy more than a single pair of shoes in any size and avoid the scam of paying twice as much for pull-ups than diapers.

Some mornings, when I'm rushing to get out the door and Joaquin has no interest in making that happen, I simply resort to what I view as conflict procrastination mode. You don't want to change out of pajamas? Fine, I'll change you in the car when we get to the day care. You don't want to stop playing with your dinosaurs? Fine, you can bring them in the car. You haven't eaten enough breakfast? Fine, I'll throw an extra granola bar into your backpack. (I say "fine" so much that he's begun to ape me with this word, including the delivery, when he reluctantly agrees to brush his teeth, clean up his puzzles, or take a nap.) The tasks of changing clothes and putting away toys become easier in the day care's parking lot, probably because he sees his school and recognizes that art, playground, and morning snack await him once he loosens himself from his demanding dad.

Parents who keep buying help in all its various forms, from advice books for themselves to martial arts classes for their kids, are engaging in a parallel game of procrastination, piling up cost after cost after cost (and, in many instances, debt after debt and debt), hopeful that the future will be easier because of these purchases. The sellers promise that their goods are laying the groundwork for that easier future, whether it's in the form of well-behaved toddlers, adolescents making responsible decisions, or young adults who can fend for themselves. These goals are, of course, desirable. They have always been desirable. Modern parents, however, are being sold on an obligation to achieve these goals in large part via spending. This panic spending is the "how" behind the $250,000 price tag per child.

5
Maddened/Melted

"Dear Andy," the note begins. "You were great! You're the best! There is no one like you! In the WORLD! Everyone wants to be like you." And then the note ends with this sign-off: "Love, Guess Who?"

My parents recently rented a dumpster so they could clean out their house, including an attic crammed with memorabilia from my childhood. Most of the attic's contents went straight into the dumpster, but my mother saved me the signing board from my Bar Mitzvah party. As was the custom in 1989, instead of a guest book, guests wrote notes to the Bar or Bat Mitzvah on a poster-sized blowup of a childhood photo. My parents used a nursery school photo of me at four years old, perched in a tree, smiling wide beneath rigid, dirty-blond bangs. Not surprisingly, many of the boys in my class ridiculed my bowl cut when signing the poster. The girls were more polite, mentioning how cute I was as a toddler before adding a "Mazel Tov" or "Congratulations" or "Have fun tonight." I don't remember signing the board myself, but my thirteen-year-old handwriting is unmistakable. I, of course, was "Guess Who."

Because I have been thinking so much about parenting, I have also, as a result, been thinking about gender dynamics. There are families in which both parents strive for a 50–50 share of responsibilities, and stay-at-home dads are becoming less and less of an anomaly. Nevertheless, parenting remains arguably the most gender-normative component of modern adulthood. Xenia and I, both physicians with busy work schedules, have tried to employ a 50–50 split of parenting, but, in truth, her share approaches something like 65 percent.

I try. I make lunches, do laundry, supervise brushing teeth, and read bedtime stories. Like the cocky thirteen-year-old who signed his Bar Mitzvah poster, I brag all the time about how much more I do for my kids than other fathers I know. Still, the division of responsibilities in our marriage is more an assignment of duties rather than an actual sharing of parental roles. In other words, Xenia is Mommy—the one whom the kids cry for when they hurt themselves, the one who cuddles with them in bed, the one who almost never yells— and I am Daddy. I'm happy to entertain them, make sure they're safe and happy and healthy, but I am also comfortable leaving the nurturing, the moral education, the true "parenting" to their mom. Indeed, the parenting books that have led me to use phrases like "moral education," the books that assume *parent* is a verb, are so obviously targeted toward mothers that, in some ways, I feel demasculinized reading them on my commuter train, with their cover images of babies and teddy bears and moms down on their knees tying their kids' shoes.

There is something more to that note I wrote myself on the night of my Bar Mitzvah than just a brace-faced, nerdy thirteen-year-old trying to build himself up. That note could only be penned by a boy, by a male. I cannot conceive of a teenage girl, or a woman of any age for that matter, even conceiving such grandiose and egotistical thoughts, let alone putting them down on a poster for all her friends and family to read. The boy is allowed to have fun and take pride in his accomplishments; the girl is not granted that same opportunity. Here I am talking as much about parenting as I am about Bar or Bat Mitzvahs. Across movies, books, television shows, and podcasts, the modern version of parenting portrayed in contemporary popular culture is vastly different for moms than for dads.

June Cleaver became Carol Brady, and Carol Brady became Clair Huxtable, and Clair Huxtable became Roseanne Conner, or maybe Marge Simpson. The through line from one generation's iconic TV mom to the next is fairly consistent. The mothers—even those who work like Clair Huxtable, a lawyer with amazingly flexible hours, and Roseanne Conner, who bounces around from one waitressing job to another—manage the household without any significant input from the fathers.

When Dad comes home at night, he is lionized for sitting down with his children and having a heart-to-heart about whatever big issue is driving the current episode. Ward Cleaver counsels Beaver on how to deal with a bully. Mike Brady tells Marcia she's beautiful despite her new set of braces, because beauty comes from within. Heathcliff Huxtable helps Vanessa nurse a broken heart after her boyfriend has cheated on her and gets Theo to see the merits of a hard-earned B in biology. Even Homer Simpson can be found asking Bart to come outside and play catch beneath an idyllic sunset to relieve some of his son's school-related stress.

None of these fathers, however, are responsible for the groceries, the laundry, the school forms, the carpools, the piano lessons, the soccer practices, the gymnastics classes, or the overdue thank you notes from last year's birthday parties. To be fair, the mothers are not usually depicted doing these things either, but there is a tacit understanding in these shows that Mom has the minutiae under control, and hence the house maintains its overall peace.

When comedian Louis C.K. premiered his television show, *Louie*, in 2010, he presented a drastically different view of domestic comedy.[1] The protagonist, a barely fictionalized version of the show's creator (he's a less successful comic who spells his first name with an "e" rather than an "s"), struggles through the daily routines of divorced fatherhood with two school-aged daughters. Louie has custody of the children during the week, while the girls' mother (almost never shown) has them on the weekends, so he can keep up the travel required of a stand-up comic. In *Louie*, we see a father trying unsuccessfully to put his daughter's hair up in pigtails, and we see the daughter yelling at the father that his ineffective combing style is hurting her. We see frantic searches for clean public bathrooms, the painful experience of listening to a child practice a new instrument, and the awkward conversations with other parents at a PTA meeting. In other words, the show makes no pretense about how awful parenthood can be.

Louis C.K. inserted into his show all the boring, tedious, and frustrating details of modern parenting. That level of honesty was an outlier not only on television but across all forms of popular media at the time. Most novels and memoirs focusing on parenthood omitted these parts of the job, under the assumption they'd come across as mind-numbingly tiresome on the page as in real life. *Louie* suffused its hyperrealistic portrayal of parenting with comedy, which perhaps softened the blow, but the other contemporary artist doing the closest thing to Louis C.K.'s work at the time, Karl Ove Knausgaard, would never be mistaken as a comic writer.

The specter of parenting hovers over the entirety of Knausgaard's six-volume work, *My Struggle*, with about equal space devoted to the author's relationship with his father and the author's relationship with his wife and children (three at the time of *My Struggle*; a fourth was born after its publication).[2] And like Louis C.K.,

Knausgaard feels no inclination toward eliding over the mundanities of raising children. In fact, his extended dives into the daily routines of parenting, with dozens of pages covering a walk to school or a trip to the grocery store to pick up last minute dinner items, seem intended to challenge his readers to keep up with him in his quest to survive the blows of fatherhood. Knausgaard's parenting stories are riveting. They are tedious at times, but they are riveting in their tediousness. James Wood, writing for the *New Yorker* on the first two volumes of *My Struggle*, summed up this phenomenon: "Even when I was bored I was interested (which is pretty much like life itself). The prose is often offensively prosaic; the scenes (such as they are) often painfully banal. Knausgaard wants his struggle to be your struggle, too; he immerses the reader in all the clumsy, extraordinary varieties of experience, from changing diapers to playing in a crappy rock band. . . . Many writers strive to give you the effect, the illusion, of reality. Knausgaard seems to want to give his readers the reality of reality."[3] By willfully acknowledging how uninteresting parenting can be, Knausgaard, like Louis C.K., has broken away from the expectations of a father, or a mother for that matter.

In her own book about motherhood, *Little Labors*, Rivka Galchen anoints Knausgaard and Louis C.K. as the most distinguished "mother writers" of the day.[4] This praise is rooted in their shared ability to address the drag that parenting can be, the way children can suck up your time, your energy, and your overall identity. In the second volume of *My Struggle*, Knausgaard famously spends nearly forty pages recounting the birthday party of his oldest daughter's classmate, and the pages are a continuous ride on the ups and downs of a parental sine wave. We start with his daughter's eager anticipation of the party (she gets to wear her gold shoes), which is matched by Knausgaard's and his wife's desire to meet more adults in their new neighborhood. Then his daughter decides, on the morning of the party, that she doesn't want to go, despite asking nearly every morning of the past week whether Stella's party was today or tomorrow. Finally, they convince her to go, but she insists on carrying her gold shoes rather than wearing them and then shies away from the other kids upon arrival. Meanwhile, Knausgaard and his wife take turns watching the children and trying, unsuccessfully, to socialize with the other moms and dads who seem to be having a much easier time as parents and as adults in general. Knausgaard eavesdrops on conversations about new television screens and vegetarian-friendly kid meals as if he's trying to decipher a foreign language (which, to some extent, is true given that the conversations are in Swedish and not his native Norwegian). By the time he finally leaves the party, late in the evening, he is as much frustrated with his daughter's behavior as he is dejected about his own performance.

Over the last decade, on every Monday of the football season, the sportswriter, Bill Simmons, and his friend,

Sal Iacono (aka Cousin Sal), record a podcast entitled *Guess the Lines*, in which the two men try to guess the point spread set by Las Vegas sportsbooks on the upcoming week's NFL games.[5] They spend about an hour going back and forth on each game and its participating teams, to the delight of the hundreds of thousands of fans (mostly male) who subscribe to their podcast. Since 2017, Simmons and Cousin Sal have added a coda to their Monday podcasts entitled "Parent Corner." The first time the two fathers introduced this segment, it came across as a lark, an accidental foray into their personal lives as each complained about the antics of their children the previous weekend. The next week, however, Simmons announced that "Parent Corner" would become a regular feature of their podcast due to popular demand. Thousands of his listeners had emailed their praise of the fathers' honesty about their parenting struggles and craved more of this content. The "Parent Corner" stories ever since have all featured a theme of frustration, whether it's Simmons's dismay at his son stealing candy from a Halloween party or Cousin Sal complaining about an elementary school scheduling a winter recital head-to-head against an important Thursday night football game.

The problem with Galchen's praise of Knausgaard and Louis C.K. as mother writers is the same problem plaguing the fathers who enjoy the "Parent Corner" segments on their football podcasts. They all—the listeners, the readers, the watchers—still exist in a world with different expectations for fathers than for mothers. An essay about "Parent Corner" in *Fatherly* uses the term "fandom parenting" to describe the tales recounted each week by Simmons and Cousin Sal.[6] These men talk about a child's obsession with slime in the same analytical way they've just discussed a quarterback's tendency to throw interceptions at the end of the first half. They observe and have vested interests in the outcome, but they don't participate. The Knausgaard on the page and the Louie on the screen do, of course, participate, but the stakes don't seem that high for these fathers, either. If Louie packs the wrong lunch, his daughter just trades it at school for something better. If Knausgaard is late to pick up his children from the day care, the teacher might give him a scolding, but it's playful, almost flirtatious.

The fathers in these popular entertainments are living in the chaotic world of parenthood (a noun, a state of being) but are not drowning in the tsunami of parenting (a verb, an effort). There's a section in Book 6 of *My Struggle* in which Knausgaard discusses a family vacation that ends with a disastrous flight home. After delineating the turmoil of dragging three sleepy kids through an airport, baggage claim, taxi line, and the drive back to their apartment, he takes a moment after all the children are finally tucked into their beds. "The last thing I did was to put Heidi's dinosaur egg in a bowl of water," he writes. "So that it would have cracked and a little dinosaur would have emerged by the time she woke the following morning." It's a beautiful image that also divulges the confidence he feels as a father. He can handle the chaos, or at least he can handle the role expected of him in this chaos.

Molly, the protagonist in Helen Phillips's *The Need*, is not feeling this brand of confidence.[7] Left alone with her two small children while her musician husband is playing a gig in South America, Molly senses an intruder in her house in the book's opening pages. Molly holds her infant son in one arm and cradles her soon-to-be-four-year-old daughter in the other. When Viv, the daughter, starts to speak, Molly cups her hand over the girl's mouth. "She remembered, for the first time in a long time, an old fear of hers from when Viv was newborn: that she would go into the baby's room in the morning after letting her cry herself back to sleep in the night only to find an empty crib with a scribble of blood on the sheet, identical to the scribble of blood where a mouse thrashed its way out of the trap on the concrete floor of the basement of her childhood home." This fear is meant to signal the guilt and anxiety Molly feels about her mothering. If that's not clear enough to the reader, we eventually learn the identity of the house's intruder is Molly herself. If not exactly Molly, then an alternate version of her, named Moll, who has arrived to both help (she dons a fish costume to entertain all of Viv's friends at her birthday party) and torment (she makes passionate love to Molly's husband when he returns home unexpectedly from his business trip) the reeling mother.

As Molly ponders her children in one of the book's early scenes, Phillips gives us a glimpse into the mother's psyche: "Moment by moment, maddened by them and melted by them, maddened/melted, maddened/melted, maddened/melted." This push-pull between enjoying and suffering through parenthood is embodied by Moll, who may or may not be real (Xenia and I had a fairly extended argument about this point, and I worry that my insistence that Moll is real says more about my gender than my reading acumen). Prior to her invasion of Molly's home, Moll has lived a parallel version of Molly's life, with a mirror husband and two children. But Moll has recently lost them to an explosion, a bomb set off at her workplace, which is essentially the same workplace as Molly's. Moll can unconditionally cherish the time she spends with Molly's family because of her loss, and only because of this loss. Before their deaths, she, like Molly, cycled through the ups and downs of motherhood, alternating between the melting and the maddening. It is no coincidence that the children die at the mother's workplace, this arena of guilt for moms who sense they should be more present for their children but know they need their own space and identity. It's hard to picture Ward Cleaver or Heathcliff Huxtable or even Karl Ove Knausgaard facing down such demons.

The Need is emblematic of recent books and films in which the chaos of parenting is sinister and monstrous for women, threatening to destroy their sanity and the family structure they've fought to build. Success—even survival—is not guaranteed for the mothers in these texts the way fathers like Louie or Bill Simmons always come out relatively unscathed at the end of their parenting tales. Before the narrator in Jenny Offill's *Dept. of Speculation* sees her marriage wrecked by her husband's affair with a much younger coworker, she watches her life crumble apart under the weight of mothering a colicky daughter she refers to as the "devil baby." The screaming of this devil baby, who can only be calmed by trips to the local Rite Aid pharmacy, rings like "a car alarm . . . perpetually going off in my head." When a well-meaning older woman on the subway uses the phrase "sleeping like a baby," the narrator confesses, "I wanted to lie down next to her and scream for five hours in her ear."[8]

In *Tully*, a film written by Diablo Cody, Marlo is a suburban mother of three whose frantic household is rescued by the arrival of Tully, a night nurse intended to help with Marlo's newborn daughter. Tully's services soon extend to the entire household, including a threesome with Marlo and her husband. The temporary bliss that Tully's presence brings to Marlo and her family is erased, however, when Tully announces she can no longer work for them. A tormented, exhausted Marlo ends up falling asleep at the wheel of her car and driving into a river, only to be saved by a mermaid-like Tully. When Marlo wakes up, she is in a psychiatric hospital, where it becomes clear that Tully never existed, and the drive into the river may have been intentional.[9] Here, as opposed to Moll in *The Need*, there is no debate about Tully's reality. We learn that Tully was Marlo's maiden name: the patient, saintly, grounded identity she relinquished for marriage and motherhood.

In *Tully*, the mother almost dies. In Leila Slimani's *The Perfect Nanny*, the children are literally sacrificed to the alter of trying to be a perfect mom.[10] Deemed the working mother's worst nightmare in its publicity material, Slimani's novel tells the story of Miriam, a lawyer with two small children, who finally is able to return to work and reclaim her identity (we are told, more than once, about how well she performed in law school and how tenacious her lawyering was prior to having children) thanks to Louise, a nanny who initially seems like Mary Poppins reincarnated. In the beginning, everything is "melted." Louise adores the children, and Miriam, relieved of the burdens of stay-at-home motherhood, gets to adore them too. But with time, the family structure, exemplified by Louise, devolves into the "maddened" component of parenting. As Louise assumes more and more of Miriam's designated role—she arrives earlier, stays later, goes on vacation with the family—she loses control. Attentiveness becomes obsession. Frustration becomes murderous rage. "The baby is dead," the book begins, and the next line describes the near-death state of the baby's older sister. We know right from page one that both children will be murdered. Slimani is not trying to conceal her outcomes or her opinions. Modern motherhood is chaotic, dangerous, and toxic.

A monstrous rage lurks in all of these popular culture depictions of mothering that would feel alien in books, shows, movies, or podcasts focused on fathers. How much of this is cultural, and how much of this is biological? And do those distinctions even matter in the twenty-first-century sport of competitive parenting? Sara Petersen, lamenting the "impossible state" of modern motherhood, writes, "In reality, mothering is not respected as 'real work.' It figures in our collective imagination not as labor, but as something warm and fuzzy and supposedly 'natural.' Maternal love and self-sacrifice are put on a pedestal by white patriarchy, but maternal work, the lifeblood of *literally everything*, is still invisible."[11] In this context, the monstrous rage in works like *The Need* and *Tully* is a clear attempt to make maternal work visible. In direct contrast to social media's (particularly Facebook and Instagram, which have been infiltrated by "momfluencer" content) portrayal of "an idealized fantasy of motherhood at odds with the lived experience of motherhood,"[12] many of today's female artists are creating works that pull back the curtain to lay bare the sometimes excruciatingly painful experience of being a mom.

The maddened/melted female protagonist is not unique to the present day. Female authors have depicted frantic women, nearly all of whom are mothers, as far back as the nineteenth century. What is unique to these modern works, however, is the direct identification of parenting—and, in some instances, the children themselves—as the source of madness. As the poet Sarah Vap writes in *Winter: Effulgences and Devotions*, her 2019 book-length exploration of how the demands of motherhood have drained her creative output, "I am losing language as my children are gaining theirs. I am losing my coherence as the children are gaining theirs. I am losing my belief in all the systems of earth just as the children are beginning to apprehend them."[13] Women in literature have lost language, coherence, and belief before. Edna Pontellier in Kate Chopin's *The Awakening* (1899),[14] Antoinette Cosway in Jean Rhys's *Wide Sargasso Sea* (1966),[15] and Sophie Blind in Susan Taubes's *Divorcing* (1969),[16] for example, all descend into some degree of madness, but the source of their descent is their marriage, their husbands, and their society's expectations of them as wives, not mothers.

The tormented wife remained the dominant "madwoman" archetype through the beginning of this century, with children often cast as minor characters bearing the brunt of their mother's madness rather than assuming any responsibility for her unhappiness. The female protagonists in Catherine Texier's *Breakup: The End of a Love Story* (1998)[17] and Elena Ferrante's *The Days of Abandoment* (2002)[18] both respond to the discovery of a husband's affair with a state of near paralysis followed by fits of intense rage directed at everyone and everything in their vicinity. This includes their children, who are depicted as innocent and undemanding, the poor victims of their mothers' crumbling under the pressure of a failed marriage. These books barely touch upon the logistics of parenting. For example, Ferrante spends more time in *The Days of Abandonment* exploring how much Olga neglects her dog, who eventually dies, than describing how she manages to raise two children on her own.

This is in stark contrast to modern titles like Julia Fine's *The Upstairs House*,[19] a horror novel about a new mother, Megan, who is haunted by the ghosts of Margaret Wise Brown, the children's book author, and Brown's lover, Michael Strange. Fine spins a surreal, frightening tale of this haunting but also manages to sprinkle in details about pumping breast milk, assembling a Pack 'n Play, and fretting about sleep schedules. "I get that people don't want to read about the adult diapers you wear after you have a baby," she said in an interview about the book, "but let's not pretend that those can't be just as literary as, you know, Philip Roth's erection."[20] *The Upstairs House* eventually turns into a painful tale of postpartum psychosis culminating in Megan's hospitalization on a mother-baby psychiatric unit and her daughter losing a finger as a result of her mother's delusions.

In Rachel Yoder's *Nightbitch*,[21] an unnamed stay-at-home mom notices a patch of hair growing on the nape of her neck and the beginnings of a tail emerging from her lower back. Her smile in the mirror reveals newly sharpened, lengthening canines. This Kafkian metamorphosis into a beastlike creature is cast as a response to the exhausting monotony (and the monotonous exhaustion) of raising her two-year-old son mostly on her own. Yoder's narrator is annoyed by her husband's absence for work trips—a similar grievance made by the mothers in *The Need* and *The Upstairs House*—but the animalistic fury that drives the book's plot is aimed squarely at maternal expectations and responsibilities. Hillary Kelly, in the *New Yorker*, writes that *Nightbitch* moves beyond more cerebral, recent novels about "white urban motherly malaise" and instead, like *The Need* and *The Upstairs House*, casts motherhood "as a force so unfathomable that it can't really be written about using the physiologic rules of our universe."[22]

The title story in Karen Russell's short story collection, *Orange World and Other Stories*, blends elements of horror and science fiction in its tale of a young expecting mother, Rae, who strikes an unusual deal with the Devil.[23] Rae is so fearful of the uncertainty awaiting her and her unborn child that she agrees to breastfeed the Devil every morning in return for the promise of her new baby's safety. The powerlessness of parents amid a realm of household terrors runs through every sentence in this story. The shocker in "Orange World" arrives when Rae finally attends a support group for mothers and divulges her painful secret. Another new mother confesses she's struck a similar deal to keep her child alive and safe. The veteran moms in the group admit they've dealt with this too. Rae has not been nurturing the Devil but a devil, like all the moms who've come before her. "Rookie mistake, babe," one of the seasoned mothers tells Rae.

When "Orange World" was published online, Twitter and Facebook lit up with comments from mothers who saw some version of themselves and their struggles in this speculative piece of fiction. The author and artist Miranda July tweeted, "For me this was a non-fiction exposé about normal, everyday life. When it was done I did the thing where u weep & have big thoughts about whole scope of your life & all the plainly obvious things you've been ignoring. They're just right there."[24] The same sort of praise thrown at Karl Ove Knausgaard and Louis C.K. for their stories about parent-teacher meetings and after-school playdates was cast, by women to a woman, for a story about a young mother losing her mind and body to a breastfeeding devil.

6
We Are Here to Help (I)

First published in 1914, *Infant Care* was one of the earliest products of the Children's Bureau, a division of the United States Department of Health, Education and Welfare created in 1912. The bureau hoped to gather, in one slender volume, the most up-to-date information on child-rearing to help new mothers and fathers. The earliest editions of *Infant Care* summarized the current literature on infant hygiene, emphasizing regularity of practices and a less emotional, more task-oriented style of parenting. Over the next four decades, *Infant Care* would grow from its original eighty-seven-page pamphlet format into a more expansive book covering more than just basic hygiene, selling millions of copies (sales estimates range from fifteen to fifty million).[1] As the book changed, so too did its author, and that change is an interesting and informative story.

The original author of *Infant Care* is identified on the booklet's cover as Mrs. Max West, a mother of five children with extensive personal experience caring for children. The choice of Mrs. West as the author of the pamphlet was reflective of the "increasingly central role accorded to women in the home and [reverence for] their innate maternity" common in the late nineteenth century.[2] However, the twentieth century saw a new breed of parenting gurus from the academic community, almost entirely male, who laid their expertise on a foundation of attacking the supposed innate knowledge of mothers and their flimsy old wives' tales. Even with Mrs. West clearly positioned as the author of *Infant Care*, the Children's Bureau employed an advisory committee of physicians (all male) to approve and endorse its contents before distributing the original edition of the booklet.

By 1919, however, this advisory panel reported they could no longer provide their expert certification to subsequent editions of *Infant Care*, already widely popular among new parents, without an author change. The panel suggested removing Mrs. West from the byline not because she was a women or a mother, but rather because she was clearly an amateur. Physicians, according to the panel's recommendation, would be more inclined to recommend the book to parents if the book had no author but rather appeared to be the collective product of the Children's Bureau and its broad assembly of child-rearing experts. As Paula Fass notes in *The End of American Childhood*, "The tide had now turned, and the expert was in the saddle." Therefore, the decision was made to lend this desired air of expertise not via a change in contents but via a change in authorship, with

Mrs. West's name no longer present on any future editions of *Infant Care*.

Mrs. Max West's ousting as the author of an influential parenting book signals a shift in attitudes about the difficulty of parenting. After all, experts are not needed for tasks that are simple. The twentieth century ushered in not only an era of parents looking for professional advice but also an era that crowned a new breed of authorities. Advances in hygiene and medical care had drastically improved infant mortality rates by this point. Once babies were expected to survive, mothers brought their healthy children into physicians' offices for advice on their mental, psychological, and cognitive well-being. In the past, these kinds of discussions, if they took place at all, were done inside the home with neighbors and grandparents and babysitters, veterans of child-rearing who could dispense simple and straightforward advice. Parents who no longer had to worry about their children's physical health now had the luxury of worrying about how best to raise these children.

Scientific authorities—physicians, psychologists, social workers—emerged to fill the gaps created by these new parental anxieties. New academic departments at prestigious universities were created to focus on child development. Scores of parenting books penned by expert authors with initials after their names began to line the bookshelves of libraries and bookstores. Parenting magazines became a new "pleasure read" for mothers (and a few fathers) looking for a less academic but still authoritative take on how to know if their children's language, emotions, and social interactions were "age-appropriate," a term that did not exist until well into the twentieth century.[3]

This brand of milestone parenting became the new standard of care for child-rearing and the dominant model under which most American children were raised until recently.[4] The twenty-first century, however, has ushered in another shift in the search for parenting experts. Parents' faith in institutions like public schools, organized religion, and the medical system to serve as safe and reliable allies in child-rearing has steadily declined over the last twenty-five years. New moms and dads, despite having been raised by parents who dogeared their copies of Dr. Spock and called their pediatricians for advice at all hours of the night, are now seeking help from unconventional sources that, on the surface, have no credentials for giving advice on teething gels, temper tantrums, bed-wetting, and sibling jealousy. If someone had told my mother to read about game theory to get her four sons to stop teasing each other, she would have laughed off the suggestion, but parents today are devouring advice books written by economists, biostatisticians, neurobiologists, investigative journalists, historians, and psychotherapists.

In *The Whole Brain Child*, Daniel Siegel and Tina Payne Bryson offer struggling parents a basic primer on the neurobiology of childhood.[5] Their review of the science behind how a child's brain forms, matures, and reacts along the journey from conception to adolescence translates decades of groundbreaking discoveries in neuroscience into easy-to-grasp messages about how humans process information related to cognitive, sensory, and motor activities. Siegel and Bryson denote the forebrain as the "upstairs brain," an area "under construction" even through the postadolescent period that, when mature, can make decisions in a balanced, respectful, and appropriate manner. Moms and dads struggling with their children are usually running up against their kids' "downstairs brains." Successful parenting, according to Siegel and Bryson, is basically teaching your children how to let the upstairs brain maintain control in good times and in bad.

The guidance conveyed in *The Whole Brain Child* is alluring because of its delivery. I likely would have paid little attention to one of Mateo's preschool teachers had she given me advice on how to control his temper by wiggling her fingers in the air and then slowly cupping them over her thumb and palm, relaying the magical effect of the sensible upstairs brain (the fingers) taming the wild and chaotic downstairs brain (the rest of the hand). When this analogy is discussed in *The Whole Brain Child*, however, the text includes evidence from functional magnetic resonance imaging (fMRI) studies and a review of the neurotransmitters involved in forebrain to midbrain communication. In other words, the advice simply sounds "smart," even to a reader like me who's well versed in the medical literature. I imagine (as a physician-scientist, I also hope) that the message would seem even "smarter" and more reliable to a non-medical parent.

And this is how I found myself sitting up on my knees, staring into Mateo's teary eyes, and exhorting him to take deep breaths to calm himself down. He was throwing clothes all around the room in protest of his favorite pants being stuck at the bottom of the dirty laundry basket. I put my left hand on his shoulder and my right hand up in the air. I waited for his eyes to drift up to my right hand and began to explain how the upstairs brain needed to regain control. "The upstairs brain knows how much you like those pants, and the upstairs brain knows that you're upset with Mommy and Daddy for not washing them yet," I said in a near whisper. "But what the upstairs brain also knows is that yelling and screaming and throwing clothes isn't going to help get those pants clean. It's smarter than your downstairs brain." His eyes lit up a bit on that last sentence. I started wiggling my fingers and slowly brought them down over my thumb and palm. "We're going to let the upstairs brain be in charge," I whispered even softer. "We'll get dressed, clean up this mess, and then we'll let Mateo do his laundry, including pouring the soap." He smiled through his tears. "Because he's in control and using his upstairs brain." I lifted up my fingers, wiggled them in the air again, and then ran them through his hair.

Can parenting be solved like a puzzle? When I experience a magical parenting moment like the one described above, relying almost verbatim on a strategy outlined for moms and dads in a book, it does seem like there are solutions for parents who know how to ask the correct questions and where to search for their answers. The influx of materials from outside fields—the neuroscience of *The Whole Brain Child*, the behavioral economics of *The Game Theorist's Guide to Parenting*,[6] the biostatistics of *Cribsheet*[7]—on the parenting sphere presumes that moms and dad can "ace" parenting, like any difficult test, if they utilize the right source materials.

The imprint of technology on this space for the current generation of parents and children is nearly impossible to understate. We have put up little fight against the screen invasion of our lives. In fact, most of us could be categorized as willing subjects to the lord of constant connectivity because this connectivity holds forth the promise of knowledge. And the promise of knowledge in turn offers the promise of power. Parents looking for help in the never-ending test of child-rearing have an infinite virtual library to peruse for answers. Sometimes these answers come in the form of an educational videogame that will keep their children quietly playing on a tablet for hours at a time. Sometimes these answers come in the form of a child-friendly restaurant recommendation from an absolute stranger. Sometimes these answers come in daily updates on a "mommy blog" with advice about toys, silverware, clothes, vacations, snacks, potty training, bottle weaning, and tapeworms.

The more exalted the source material, the more appealing the advice is to savvy consumers like today's parents. The other night, Xenia was reading an article on education in preparation for a medical student class she was teaching. "This is a good quote," she said, and then proceeded to read aloud, "Little is taught by contest or dispute, everything by sympathy and love." She looked up from her phone and waited for my approval. "It's from Samuel Taylor Coleridge," she said. "As in Coleridge, the poet?" I asked. "Apparently, he delivered a famous lecture on education once," she said. "Makes a lot of sense for our kids, though, doesn't it?" she added. I asked her to take a screenshot of the Coleridge quote and text it to me, so I could save it to my phone's camera roll. Someday I'd refer back to Coleridge's advice, and it would help that the advice came from Coleridge.

Indeed, the further distance experts put between themselves and conventional parenting gurus lends them a respected, outsider status that aligns with the current business model of seeking help from an impartial, external advisor. Just as distressed companies utilize consulting firms to improve their performance, distressed parents can utilize the knowledge of an external consultant to deal with their children. Kevin Zollman, the coauthor of *The Game Theorist's Guide to Parenting: How the Science of Strategic Thinking Can Help You Deal with the Toughest Negotiators You Know—Your Kids*, is a professor at Carnegie Mellon University who had a running column in the *Pittsburgh Post-Gazette* discussing how game theory applied to various aspects of our social lives (e.g., how stores price their products and how people choose their life partners). When asked by a mainstream publisher to write a game theory–focused book on parent-child conflicts, Zollman initially expressed disbelief that he, a philosophy professor with no children, could stand as a parenting expert. In an interview with his university newsletter, Zollman explains that this is why he requested a more conventional coauthor in Paul Raeburn, a science writer with five kids.[8]

The childless professor's advice on two siblings arguing over who gets to be the first one to try out a new video game is worlds away from Mrs. Max West's motherly suggestions on teething pains and diaper rashes. And it's not just the author who has changed but the advice itself. Zollman and Raeburn, for the above-mentioned problem of who gets to go first, suggest using an auction system, in which each kid announces how much they'd be willing to pay for the opportunity to be first. Payment here would not be in the form of money but rather household chores or hours spent quietly reading or weekly phone calls to grandparents. As with *The Whole Brain Child* and its breakdowns of neuroscience, the advice dished out in *The Game Theorist's Guide to Parenting* assumes an air of authority by translating the seemingly hard concepts of behavioral economics into bite-sized nuggets that parents can understand and immediately employ.

Emily Oster's books may be the apotheosis of the shift in what has come to be understood as modern parenting expertise. Oster has already penned two best sellers—*Expecting Better*,[9] which focuses on pregnancy and childbirth, and *Cribsheet*, which covers the years from birth to preschool—with a third book, *The Family Firm*,[10] on the early school years, published in 2021 (and, like its predecessors, expected to be another best seller). Oster is a mom but her position as a parenting expert is rooted firmly in her other job as an economist and professor at Brown University. She teaches parents how to think about choices much the same way she teaches her college-aged students to think about economics problem sets: explore the upsides and downsides of an issue, formulate a decision-making process that is informed by the best available information, take action, and then evaluate objectively the effects of that action.

The best available information, for Oster and her now devoted fan base, lies in data. Oster is an economist, but she is tapping into the same hot spring of numbers and statistics that folks like Nate Silver, Bill James, and Steven Levitt have used for popular culture takes on politics, sports, and the real estate market. Oster's relatively unemotional, objective analyses of the available data on child-rearing are smart, succinct, and, perhaps most importantly, often reassuring. Many of Oster's examinations—whether it's naps or nutrition or night-time baths—end up in the same place, with the stats supporting a variety of approaches. In some ways, Oster is the heir apparent to the throne once held by Dr. Spock and his famous "Trust yourself" mantra, albeit with a modern twist. She extols parents to trust themselves, but she does so with a healthy supply of statistical output to appease parents who may not feel comfortable trusting themselves but are more than ready to trust an Ivy League professor's research.[11]

"The desire to consume is a kind of lust," Lewis Hyde once wrote.[12] If modern parenting is a game of competitive shopping, as discussed in chapter 4, then the evolution of the parenting expert to include outside consultants was inevitable. Parents don't just need *some* advice. They need *all* the advice, especially the kind that comes with impressive credentials and a bit of exculpatory comfort. It's not your fault that your kids are trying to murder each other. Their brains have not yet been wired to control their emotions, or they're just like any two entities with competing interests, or they'll grow out of their sibling rivalry according to pretty much every well-done study in the scientific literature. In a recent essay for *The Riveter*, Kimberly Seals Allers voices concerns about this trend and how it devalues the work of parenting, specifically mothering. "Instead of turning to mothers and grandmothers with generations of wisdom about child rearing or trusting our maternal cues," she writes, "we are told data and science are meant to be our primary parenting guides." Parents today seem eager and willing to hand over their autonomy to "a new overseer: a scientific report."[13]

It's hard to read Philippa Perry's *The Book You Wish Your Parents Had Read (and Your Children Will Be Glad That You Did)*[14] without thinking of the warnings voiced by Seals Allers. Perry's book strikes, on the surface, a similar tone as conventional parenting books. Its main message is empathy, which is par for the course in this genre. Perry is not a child psychologist but rather a psychotherapist whose prior books were a graphic novel about the relationship between a therapist and one of her clients (*Couch Fiction*, 2010) and an academia-meets-mainstream book on maintaining good mental health (*How to Stay Sane*, 2012). She therefore discusses empathy not as a parent but as a psychotherapist. She begins with a bit of tough love for the anxious moms and dads who have turned to her book, arguing that their problems being a "good" parent stem from their own parents' inability to understand and support them in a mutually respectful relationship. Perry urges her readers to "mirror" and "validate" their children's feelings to break this cycle—otherwise, their children will eventually find fewer and fewer healthy ways to express themselves. She asks parents to examine their own reactions to their children and ask if their anger, distress, and anxiety stems from their children's behavior or something childlike and unfulfilled in themselves.

For a book with such a catchy title, *The Book You Wish Your Parents Had Read* is a tough read for moms and dads, especially if they start page one without any resentment toward their own parents. Yet who can say Perry is wrong? Maybe the only authorities who could call out these new parenting experts—whether they hail from the field of psychotherapy, economics, or neuroscience—as emperors without clothes are the previous generations of parents who never needed this kind of outsider input. "You want to be the person your child can talk to," Perry advises parents. Today's distressed moms and dads probably aren't talking to their own parents about the unconventional books they're scouring for advice. And that lack of conversation only confirms Perry's theories.

7
We Are Here to Help (II)

Jason notices me sitting on the couch after he's taken his first bite of a Snickers. He smiles and offers a half wave before heading to the stairway. His face betrays embarrassment. It's just after 5:00 p.m., and he is obviously sating some predinner hunger pangs via the lobby's vending machines. I hope he doesn't think I'm judging him on his choice of snack. I frequently grab a bag of chips from one of the hospital's vending machines to push through the last hour or two of a long workday. Taking care of people is hard work, and caregivers deserve a little junk food in return. His scarfing down a candy bar and then rushing back upstairs to work with my four-year-old son shouldn't make either of us uncomfortable.

Jason is either a physical therapist or an occupational therapist. I should know his title, but TheraPlay makes a point of stressing a care team rather than individual practitioners. On Monday afternoons, Mateo works with a group of physical and occupational therapists as part of his early intervention program for sensory integration disorder. Rosemary is the occupational therapist who greets

Mateo and me in the waiting room and walks Mateo back to the facility's gymnasium, but once inside Mateo "plays" with her and Jason and a half dozen other therapists. At the end of his session, Rosemary brings Mateo back to the waiting room. I sign a form documenting that Mateo has received his early intervention services, while she tells me what a fun time they've just had crawling through resistance tunnels, writing his name with coffee beans, and mastering new yoga poses.

Mateo's difficulties at home and in preschool apparently stem from his brain's inability to receive and respond to information that comes in through the senses.[1] Rosemary, Jason, and the rest of the care team at TheraPlay are trying to retrain Mateo's brain so that he no longer slaps his baby brother on the back as part of his routine morning greeting. He's doing handstands and crab walks so that he'll learn he can't always be first in line for recess. He's sculpting balls out of a super-thick version of Play-Doh called therapy putty so that other kids want to have playdates with him.

TheraPlay takes up about half of the third floor of an otherwise nondescript office building. The other half of the floor, in a heaping dose of unintentional irony, belongs to a geriatrics physical therapy office. As Mateo sprints down the carpeted hallway toward TheraPlay, he usually has to weave his body, like a slalom skier, around octogenarians shuffling toward their own gym on crutches or walkers. "Mateo, slow down," I say for their benefit, wearing an apologetic smile. Once inside the waiting room, Mateo takes off his socks and shoes before hiding under my chair. We wait for Rosemary to emerge. We wait for me to say the same thing each time. "I'm sorry, but I forgot to bring Mateo." We wait for him to jump out and yell, "Surprise!" And then I watch Rosemary lead him back to the gym, knowing I have forty-five minutes to myself.

Just a few weeks into his life, Xenia started to notice an abnormal appearance to Mateo's stools and wondered if his crankiness was related to some sort of allergy. Her mother, who'd been staying with us since the day after Mateo's birth, identified him as a colicky baby from the start and was giving him a nightly bottle of diluted chamomile tea, a Mexican remedy that did nothing for his screaming fits. Xenia began scouring websites to decipher why his stools had such an odd texture and color, and thus began a series of visits to our pediatrician and, eventually, a pediatric immunologist who diagnosed Mateo with FPIES, food protein-induced enterocolitis syndrome. Xenia would have to cut out dairy and soy and eggs from her diet to keep his allergies in check. Even with these measures, he had specks of blood in his stool, diffuse outbreaks of eczema over his face and scalp, and an inability to sit still in anyone's arms other than Xenia's. She made oatmeal masks for his skin and kept meticulous diaries about the contents of his diaper.

Driving home after one of his doctor's appointment, Xenia said, "I feel guilty, like maybe we've done the wrong thing. Maybe I shouldn't have cut out milk. Maybe I shouldn't have cut out soy. Maybe we should have just forced him to adapt to those foods. I don't want him to be this ultrasensitive kid." I reminded her how fussy Mateo had been before she cut out those foods, and how much happier he seemed now. "In Mexico, there's no way they're asking moms to get rid of milk and soy and gluten," Xenia countered. "And the kids there turn out fine." I told her Mateo would be fine. "Why does every kid in America need a diagnosis?" she responded.

The rush to give every kid a diagnosis—or, in the least, a label—extends beyond just gastrointestinal symptoms. Consider all the books on sleep training and the new profession of "sleep coaches" that have problematized normal infant sleep variations.[2] Or all the parents who casually throw around the term "on the spectrum" to frame their worries about their children's verbal output, shyness around strangers, and difficulty making friends.[3] Or the rush to diagnose any child struggling in school with attention deficit disorder (ADD).[4] Today's children are not unequivocally different from children fifty years ago, yet they carry diagnoses at an alarmingly high rate. In Mateo's preschool classroom, for example, six of the eighteen students had been identified for early intervention with a special education itinerant teacher assigned to them for certain hours of the day.

Academic and economic pressures explain much of the rush to diagnose today's children, with these pressures perceived more by their parents than by the children themselves. Children now go to school longer than ever before. As a result, the schooling requirements for nearly all occupations have become more and more demanding. Children who can't succeed at academic learning face major disadvantages not just in school but in the job market that awaits them after they complete their studies. The increased emphasis on school-based achievements as the route to a prosperous—or at least secure—future parallels the epidemic of attention deficit disorder in the United States, where the condition has been diagnosed more than in any other country.[5] The ADD label, or its variant of ADHD (adding hyperactivity to the mix), can serve as an explanation for the failure of children who are not willing or able to put up with the quiet and concentration demanded in schools. Not surprisingly, anxious American parents have invested heavily in diagnosing and controlling the disorder, including frequent use of stimulant medications like methylphenidate (Ritalin) in kindergarteners through graduate students.

Sensory integration disorder is a relative newcomer compared to ADD and ADHD. The diagnosis is not listed in the *Diagnostic and Statistical Manual of Mental Disorders* (*DSM*) published by the American Psychiatric Association,[6] and the American Academy of Pediatrics has recommended that pediatricians not use sensory integration disorder (or sensory processing disorder, the other commonly used nomenclature) as a stand-alone diagnosis.[7] Occupational therapist Jean Ayres first introduced the concept of sensory processing difficulties in the early 1970s, arguing that certain people's brains couldn't process all the information coming in through the seven senses to provide a clear representation of both their external and internal worlds.[8] Dr. Ayres cited seven and not the traditional five senses of touch, taste, hearing, smell, and sight. The "internal" senses of proprioception—body awareness—and vestibular drive—movement—were equally and often more prone to defective processing in some children.[9]

The description of sensory integration disorder seems deliberately vague, almost as if it were intentionally designed to be as inclusive as possible of all childhood misbehavior or struggles. Some of the characteristic signs and symptoms of sensory integration disorder, such as aversion to certain fabric textures or significant discomfort induced by relatively mild deviations in ambient temperature, are quite specific to "sensory kids" and feel like a more legitimate indicator of the diagnosis than the slew of other behaviors often attributed to the disorder.[10] Fidgeting, impulsiveness, yelling, aversion to pungent foods, and prolonged temper tantrums have all been listed in articles and books describing sensory processing defects, but these common misbehaviors have also been staples of parent-child struggles long before moms and dads were prompted to consider their child's body awareness.

When Mateo is off with his TheraPlay team working on his sensory processing, I spend my forty-five minutes in the waiting room trying to read a book. On a good day, I might get through ten pages. Reading in the waiting room is a challenge because, at any point in time, at least three or four children are waiting to be called in by their own version of Rosemary. Many of these kids, I presume based on the volume of their voices and their disregard for others' personal spaces, carry the same sensory integration disorder diagnosis as Mateo. These kids tend to be boys and are the types that would have been labeled "hyper" or "wild" or even just "annoying" when I was growing up.

It's hard to read because of the other children *and* their parents. If I'm not distracted by the sound of a five-year-old hysterically crying, then I'm watching his mother try to manage the scene he's making. These are the boys who are doing worse than Mateo and the parents who are struggling much harder than me. The boys can only tolerate twenty- or thirty-minute sessions with the therapy team, and they often scream and kick when their therapists come to get them. They refuse to take off their coats or hats or socks or shoes. They sometimes latch on to chairs and force their parents and therapists to pry them loose. The moms and dads react poorly according to the parenting books: They make threats ("No dessert tonight") or resort to bribes ("Double dessert tonight"). They disparage their children to their faces ("Why can't you just cooperate for once?") or in conversations with the therapists ("He's been impossible all day long"). When their children are finally out of the waiting room, they spend their free time sighing, biting their nails, and looking at their phones. It's hard not to wonder whether sensory integration disorder, a diagnosis whose prevalence has grown exponentially in the past decade, was conceived to make parents like us feel less guilty about how our children are faring.

Henry's mother is the exception in the TheraPlay waiting room. Henry must be six or seven based on his height. He almost always enters in the arms of his mother. She's no more than five foot three, with a bob cut and slender frame, and her son likely weighs just fifteen or twenty pounds less than she does. They have matching hairstyles, and their cheeks carry the same rosy glow, his I presume from sensitive skin, hers more from the exertion of lugging this boy in her arms as he shouts directly into her ears. She keeps him pressed up against her body as she settles into a chair, holding him tight in his distress until Jason, TheraPlay's only male therapist, comes to take him. Henry's mother never raises her voice. I don't hear exactly what she's saying to her son, because she speaks in a whisper, the ideal volume for a sensory child. Henry slithers out of his mother's arms directly into Jason's. The screaming continues, this time into Jason's ears. When Henry's out of the waiting room, his mother doesn't betray any frustration or disappointment with him. The only concession she gives is bending over to touch her toes, then reaching up both arms toward the ceiling, and, finally, using both hands to massage her lower back.

The other parents and their children present a chicken-and-egg dilemma: are the moms and dads "parenting" so ineffectively and counterproductively because their children are difficult, or are the children difficult because their parents are failing at their basic duties? Henry's pixie-like mother and her saintly presence in the waiting room inspire no such questioning. I see myself in the other parents, not in Henry's mother, although I have been working hard to change and be more like her. The stack of parenting books and articles printed out from child development websites on my bedside table attests to this effort. I still blow up at Mateo when he misbehaves. I still feel frustration boiling up inside me when he refuses to cooperate. But I do this less and less. I try to whisper. I put my hands gently on his shoulders. And when all that fails, I hold him upside down.

In the waiting room, perhaps as a way to distinguish myself from the other non-Henry-affiliated parents, perhaps as a way to gain points with Henry's mother, I deliberately model the good parenting prescribed by all the books I'm reading. I lead with empathy and speak softly when Mateo is upset. "You seem very angry today," I sing-speak in a Mary Poppins-esque tone. "I can tell you're having a hard time right now." I then gently set limits. "The problem is we're here for therapy, and we only have a short time each week with Rosemary." I wait for Mateo to understand that I am here to help and not oppose before proposing a solution. "On the ride home after therapy, should we listen to 'Pop See Ko' or an Abba song?"

Henry walks into the waiting room today, holding his mom's hand. They're talking about snowmen. I pretend to keep reading but watch them over the top of my book. Henry takes a seat on the chair beside his mother. She keeps hold of his hand and playfully asks him questions about how he'd decorate his imaginary snowman. I recognize the anxious look on her face and the stagey sound of her voice, the signs of a parent who's having a quiet and peaceful experience with a troubled child and is trying her best to keep the moment intact. She's working, but this interaction is a much easier task than carrying his large body in her arms. Her cheeks still blaze red, as do Henry's, but this time I figure she's blushing from the excitement of their conversation and the calm in their corner of the waiting room. "Here's Jason," she says when their therapist comes to take Henry. She announces Jason's entrance with a note of disappointment, or maybe it's concern, that this happy episode is about to end. Henry takes Jason's hand and walks into the gym. I keep watching his mom. She's suppressing a grin. She paws at her cheeks and then rubs her hands together, as if her body needs something to do without a backache to nurse.

My phone buzzes to remind me that I'm scheduled to join a conference call for work. I leave the room and head down to the lobby. A few weeks ago, a new sign at

TheraPlay announced their intentions to create a "sensory friendly" waiting room. Parents were requested not to use electronic devices in the waiting room while children were present. Thus far, the only two parents I've seen respect this request are me and Henry's mom, but we were the only two who read books even before the sign went up. I've seen her leave the waiting room to answer her phone, though, and so I put in my earbuds and dial into the conference call from the lobby, proud of my contribution to TheraPlay's sensory-friendly environment.

It's nice to be out of the waiting room. I normally hate conference calls, but I lean back into the lobby's black leather couch, put my phone on mute, and listen to a fairly unimportant conversation among my colleagues. I contribute minimally when called upon, but for the most part I'm silent and not paying close attention. I rest my head on the soft couch cushions, close my eyes, and wonder why I haven't been spending every session down here in the lobby, on this comfortable couch, in this quiet space where I don't need to deal with unmanageable kids and disgruntled parents and the guilt of knowing that someone like Henry's mom is contending with so much more than I am and doing such a better job than I ever could.

In between sessions, I've often questioned whether Mateo's issues are overblown, whether he's been misdiagnosed and lumped into a category he doesn't really fit. He may just be weird, the way I was weird when I was his age. I sometimes licked windows or pushed my forehead up against the refrigerator door as he repeatedly does now. I didn't insist on wearing long-sleeve shirts and sweatpants in the peak of summer like Mateo does, but that too could be called "odd" rather than "sensory seeking." In the waiting room, however, when I see Henry and the other children lose control, I remember the way Mateo bites his arms or violently scratches his knees, to the point of bleeding, when he's angry. In the waiting room, I know that my son is behaving so much better than before he started receiving his early intervention services, but he's still not acting completely "normal," whatever that word is supposed to mean. In the waiting room, I watch the other parents and feel guilty about how much I dislike having to come here each week and how I sometimes wish my son was more like other children his age. In the lobby, however, I can simply take a phone call or read a book or take a nap without any concern other than whether my son's therapist thinks I'm judging him for his choice of snack.

At 5:13 p.m., I drop the conference call so that I'm back in the waiting room when Rosemary brings Mateo out after his session. "Where were you?" Mateo asks. Rosemary explains that Mateo had to use the bathroom during his appointment, and they looked for me in the waiting room to take him. "He was pretty upset because he didn't want a girl to take him," Rosemary says, using a childish voice to include Mateo in our discussion.

"But once we did a few calming exercises, we realized that Jason could take him." I apologize and explain that I needed to take a phone call in the lobby. "I was crying, Daddy," Mateo says. Rosemary says it's no big deal, he got himself under control very quickly. She asks that I just let the secretary know if I'm not going to be in the waiting room during a session.

The embarrassment on Jason's face had nothing to do with a Snickers bar. His awkward smile and half wave were his way of acknowledging he'd just taken my son to the bathroom because I was nowhere to be found. But then he did find me—in the lobby, lounging on a couch with my legs splayed out. I was wearing earbuds for my call, and he probably thought I was listening to a podcast or playlist. He probably knew I was congratulating myself on having escaped the waiting room and the wayward children to whom he's devoted his career. I apologize again to Rosemary and remind her of the conference call and the waiting room's sensory-friendly rules. "Please tell Jason," I say before promising this won't happen again.

Once we've left the waiting room, Mateo starts his sprint to the elevator. Up ahead of us, a white-haired man, whose right knee is bound up in an enormous brace, is limping toward the elevator with a four-pronged quad cane. "Mateo!" I cry out. "Mateo! No!" Mateo stops in his tracks and turns around. He's just had his hair buzzed short, so his face is all eyes and big smile.

Rosemary suggested that Xenia and I try our best to cut the word "no" out of our communications with Mateo. "The words 'no' and 'don't' can be very intimidating to someone like Mateo," Rosemary said, "because he hears what he can't do but isn't encouraged to do what he can. If he hears 'speak quietly' instead of 'don't yell,' he will feel reassurance about how he can interact with others." The advice was like so many of the suggestions given to parents of sensory kids: a warm, friendly maneuver that likely would benefit any child but might have particularly strong effects on a kid in turmoil.

"Mateo," I say again, but softer, as I soak in those eyes and that smile.

"What, Daddy?"

"Want to race?"

8
Parents Strike Back

Whenever a colleague at work announces that they are expecting their first child, I always recommend the same two books for their prenatal reading: *On Becoming Babywise*[1] and *Secrets of the Baby Whisperer*.[2] I suggest they start with *Babywise*, which advocates putting newborns on a regimented schedule in which they eat for thirty minutes every three hours, then are deliberately kept awake for another thirty minutes, and then are put down for a two-hour sleep. The cycle is repeated around the clock over the first two weeks. By week 3, the last feed can be given just before parents go to bed. There's no need to wake up the baby, who should sleep uninterrupted for the next seven or eight hours. And by week 8 or 12, the last feed can be given much earlier in the night, well before the parents go to bed, so that the parents can actually have some pleasurable time together and regain their nights by themselves.

My expecting colleagues say they'll do whatever it takes to have their babies sleep through the night, but invariably they all return to me after reading *Babywise* claiming they can't go through with the book's training schedule. The techniques work, I counter, and working parents need to protect their own sleep and their own schedules. I then suggest they try the *Baby Whisperer*, which promotes an almost identical schedule to *Babywise* but does so with much softer language. Those who go on to read the *Baby Whisperer* typically come back later saying they will give sleep training a chance.

The overarching message of *Babywise*, which can be off-putting to a couple who is expecting their first child, is to place the interests of the family above the interests of the baby. In virtually all instances, the interests of the family translate to the interests of the parents. The *Babywise* books began as a short pamphlet entitled *Parent Controlled Feeding* penned by Anne Marie Ezzo for parenting classes she and her husband, Gary, were leading in their evangelical megachurch. In 1990, the Ezzos expanded upon this small tract and self-published *Preparation for Parenting: Bringing God's Order to Your Baby's Day and Restful Sleep to Your Baby's Night*, which is essentially a first draft of what would eventually become *Babywise*. Their church, initially supportive of the publication and their parenting ministry, eventually banned the book for alienating parents who favored more traditional child-rearing methods like demand feeding for newborns, co-sleeping with infants, and using sling-type baby carriers. In the announcement of this ban, the church elders criticized the Ezzos for "stifling the mother's desire to comfort her children" and misusing biblical texts to justify their parenting philosophy. Sleep training can require parents to leave a crying infant alone for up to thirty minutes, an act that the Ezzos compared to the cruxification of Jesus ("Praise God that the Father did not intervene when His Son cried out on the cross").[3]

Gary Ezzo eventually teamed up with a pediatrician, Robert Bucknam, to pen a secular version of his and his wife's suggestions, now titled *On Becoming Babywise*, which first appeared in 1993 with later editions published in 1998, 2001, and 2007. Despite the book's commercial success, its emphasis on parental control of the infant's schedule, rather than allowing the baby to decide when to eat and sleep, was met with opposition from both parent and physician groups who voiced concerns that the *Babywise* techniques put children at increased risk for malnutrition, failure to thrive, and developmental disorders. The American Academy of Pediatrics put forth a statement highlighting the contrast between the *Babywise* schedule of feeds and their own recommendations on nursing newborns.[4] The growing criticism lobbed against *Babywise* was, ironically, paralleled by an influx of parenting books promising the same kind of feed and sleep training in packaging far friendlier to new parents (and their pediatricians). This competition was probably at least as important as the rebukes from physician groups in leading to the *Babywise* books going out of print.

Secrets of the Baby Whisperer is a fascinating read if you've just finished reading *Babywise*, which is why I recommend the books in that order. In the *Baby Whisperer*, Tracy Hogg, a nurse specializing in maternity and neonatal care, writing alongside journalist Melinda Blau, passes along the wisdom she's learned from her nursing career and her own experiences raising two daughters to help parents put a happy baby to sleep through the night. The key to "baby whispering" begins with a catchy acronym—E.A.S.Y.—that lays out a schedule for parents to follow. E is for eat, A is for awake, S is for sleep, and Y is for your time. The E.A.S.Y. schedule should be repeated every 2.5 to 3.5 hours—meaning the child should be fed about every three hours, followed by fun awake time for thirty minutes, and then sleep for two hours, during which period the parents can do whatever they need to do (sleep themselves, clean a room, take a shower, or clink wine glasses).

The schedule is, of course, identical to that put forth in *Babywise*, but the reason why the *Baby Whisperer* has remained in print while *Babywise* fell to the used book bin sits entirely in each book's style and delivery. The *Baby Whisperer* uses the softest possible language, referring to babies *and* parents as "loves," and presents the E.A.S.Y. schedule as a way parents can connect with— "whisper to"—their children. Hogg and Blau promise their readers that getting their infants onto the E.A.S.Y. schedule will make their children happier. They allude to the happiness of the parents, of course, but they do not lead with that intention. The book is baby-focused. In contrast, every sentence in *Babywise* marches to the same drumbeat: parents can address their needs and their children's needs simultaneously, principally by focusing on what they—and not their children—want.

The demise of *Babywise* may simply be a case of poor timing, as the book ran up directly against the wave of helicopter parenting that became popular during the 1990s and 2000s. The term "helicopter parent" was first used in a 1969 book, *Between Parent and Teenager*, in which a teenager complains that his mother watches over him like a helicopter.[5] But the term did not fall into common parlance until the turn of the century, when watching over children like a helicopter was no longer considered negative behavior in some parenting circles. The idea of getting a child onto a sleeping and eating schedule, in theory, should align with the practices of helicopter parents who are often accused of overscheduling their children's activities, but the ethos of helicopter parenting is one of "children-first" whereas *Babywise* preached a "parents-first" philosophy.

In 2019, a new, updated edition of *Babywise* came back into print. The cover of this new edition, coincidentally or not, uses a near replica of the color schemes for the *Baby Whisperer* series. And the text in the new *Babywise* has been modified from the older, out-of-print editions, in part to address new parenting challenges that have arisen since the original iterations of the book (e.g., should infants be allowed to play with iPads) but also in part to employ the same kind of child-friendly approach its successors used so well. Still, the message of the book remains intact—happy children spring from happy (and rested) parents who feel that they have control of the family's interests. The reissue was a success, as evidenced by another reissue of *Babywise* in 2020 marking its thirtieth anniversary.[6]

The *Babywise* comeback story again may come down to timing—this time of the propitious sort—in that the last decade has seen a growing backlash against helicopter parenting and child-centered families. David Code's best seller, *To Raise Happy Kids, Put Your Marriage First*, exemplifies this shift.[7] Code, a family therapist, argues, "Today's number one myth about parenting is that the more attention we give our kids, the better they'll turn out. But we parents have gone too far: our over-focus on our children is doing them more harm than good." Adults should spend less time trying to be the perfect parents and more time striving to be the perfect spouses if they want to raise happy, well-adjusted, and generally non-annoying children. In Code's own words: "Families centered on children create anxious, exhausted parents and demanding, entitled children." His book exhorts parents not to sacrifice their lives for their kids. This parents-first message aligns perfectly with *Babywise*'s core principles and has found an audience of sympathetic listeners in moms and dads desperate to regain control of their own days and nights while not sacrificing their children's outcomes.

Pamela Druckerman's *Bringing Up Bébé: One American Mother Discovers the Wisdom of French Parenting* is another recent best seller plugging a less-is-more, parent-centered approach for struggling American parents.[8] Druckerman claims to have found the secret to well-behaved and well-adjusted children by studying the mores of French moms and dads, who let their babies cry themselves to sleep and refuse to create a separate menu for their toddlers. The French parents expect their children to eat, sleep, and play on a schedule that mirrors their parents' routines. There's no constant snacking, for example, and children who claim they're "starving" at 10:30 a.m. are asked politely to wait until the family's set lunchtime. The curtains and blinds are drawn open when children nap to note the distinction between a short daytime snooze and nighttime, when they should be sleeping uninterrupted for ten to twelve hours.

Druckerman marvels at how much happier French moms and dads are than their American counterparts, reporting with envy how much sleep French parents get, how often they socialize with other adults, and how frequently they have sex. Parents who read *Bringing Up Bébé* and feel the same envy that Druckerman herself did watching French kids eat braised leeks and play by themselves while their contented parents leisurely sipped café au lait need to examine how child-centric their families have become. As *Fatherly* magazine's glowing review of *Bringing Up Bébé* concludes, "Don't let the [children] think they're the center of the universe (even if they're the center of your universe)."[9]

The moms and dads who have bought into the "parents first" message may be the same ones who have become enamored by the recent "free-range" parenting movement that encourages a more laissez-faire approach to child-rearing. Positioned directly in contrast, and as a reaction, to the previous generation of helicopter parents, free-range parents are the new "hip" moms and dads who boast about their children's independence, maturity, and confidence bred from granting these children responsibilities, with less and less parental intervention, from a young age.[10]

The birth of the free-range parenting movement, by most accounts, was a 2008 article by *New York Sun* columnist Lenore Skenazy that described the benefits of letting her nine-year-old son ride the New York City subway system alone.[11] Despite the backlash this article received (Skenazy was dubbed "America's Worst Mom" by more than one publication), Skenazy felt empowered by the positive responses she heard from parents who wanted the same kind of independence in their and their children's lives. She went on to write a best seller, *Free-Range Kids: How to Raise Safe, Self-Reliant Children (Without Going Nuts with Worry)*,[12] and start the Let Grow Project aimed at a large-scale cultural shift that applauds, rather than rebukes, adults for allowing children to experiment with and perform tasks without supervision.

Free-range parents who let their kids ride their bikes to the park or walk alone to school can feel empowered by science and epidemiology in their pushback against the prevailing culture of parental overprotection and overinvolvement. Animal studies have shown that free play promotes development of neurons along the pathways of the prefrontal cortex, strengthening this area of the brain's control over the emotional responses elicited by the limbic system. In children, risky play and its associated thrilling experiences, when viewed from an evolutionary psychology perspective, are required elements of growing up due to their antiphobic effects, fostering exposure and coping responses to stimuli they have been bred to fear (e.g., heights or strangers).[13] The decline in children's freedom to play over the past fifty years has been matched by increases in their responses on standardized questionnaires indicating depression (eightfold higher now) and/or anxiety (five- to tenfold higher, depending on the scale). Child psychologists who advocate for some version of free-range parenting stress how important it is for children of all ages to feel that they have some control over their decisions and lifestyle.[14]

The free-range parenting philosophy is no longer a fringe movement but now a fashionable and accepted way for modern parents to choose a child-rearing style that is the opposite of the uber-involved and uber-unhappy helicopter parenting. The popularity of this independent parenting style has forced states to catch up with their child neglect laws, with Utah being the first to explicitly legalize free-range parenting. The 2018 Utah bill, colloquially dubbed the "free-range parenting" law, was unanimously passed by both chambers of Utah's legislature and fundamentally changed the state's legal definition of neglect, allowing "a child, whose basic needs are met and who is of sufficient age and maturity to avoid harm or unreasonable risk of harm, to engage in independent activities." A similar bill was introduced in South Carolina shortly thereafter, and now nine states have been classified by the Let Grow Project as having laws that protect rather than punish children's independence.[15]

In a *New Yorker* cartoon by Sophia Wiedeman, two women sit on a couch enjoying their coffee while a small child plays behind them unattended. The toddler is sitting underneath a crookedly hung painting, just beside an open book whose pages have been ripped out, breaking her crayons in half. The wall behind her is spotted with her small handprints, and in front of her lies a teddy bear who seems to have died of neglect. The cartoon's caption is a bit of dialogue between the two women on the couch: "I can never tell if I'm allowing independent play or just ignoring her."[16]

So many of the articles and posts about the benefits of free-range parenting invoke a "good old days" when kids stayed out riding their bikes or playing ball until the streetlights came on, signaling a natural (and not adult-enforced) end of the day. This nostalgia for the "good old days" strikes two different chords for today's parents—a desire for their kids to enjoy the same freedoms and thrills they experienced as children, and a wish for themselves to enjoy the same guilt-free, hands-off, time-to-myself parenting style their mothers and fathers seemed to employ without consequence. Wiedeman's cartoon has relevance to the free-range discussion because the mother on the couch is all smiles even as she frets over whether she's really just getting away with ignoring her daughter.

Both women in the cartoon, like the overwhelming majority of parents who subscribe to the free-range movement, are white, and this raises another pitfall not just for free-ranging but for all of the parents-first philosophies that have emerged in the past decade. In many instances, the distinction between independent play versus neglect is subjective, with race and class influencing such judgement. In an essay in *The Atlantic* entitled "'Free Range' Parenting's Unfair Double Standard," Jessica McCrory Calarco argues that "for some parents—poor and working-class parents, and especially poor and working-class parents of color— free-range parenting has long been a necessity, even if it didn't previously get the virtuous-sounding label it has today."[17] Parents from low-income households who work full time, particularly if they are single parents, often have no choice but to leave their kids at home and task them with responsibilities like making dinner and buying this week's groceries. Calarco worries that the poor and working-class parents who have the most to gain from the free-range parenting movement will find themselves held to a different set of expectations than the better-educated and better-paid parents who have the time and freedom to post photos on Facebook of their kids heading off on their own to elementary school. Most free-range parents haven't considered the privileges they have that allow them to espouse this child independence movement. Like the mom in Wiedeman's cartoon, they are simply too excited by their own, newfound independence.

9
Precision Parenting

On the short walk from the train station to the hospital, I saw a street sweeper a few feet ahead of me. I picked up my pace to catch up to the giant vehicle and waited for its driver to notice me frantically waving at him. Charles smiled when he saw me and rolled down the street sweeper's version of a passenger side window. The vehicle moved so slowly that he never actually stopped driving and sweeping.

"Good morning, Doc!" he yelled over the noise.

"Good to see you!" I yelled back.

He rolled up the window, we both waved at each other, and then I gave him a thumbs up sign. He flashed a huge grin and returned his focus to the street ahead of him. His face looked fatter than when I'd last seen him, but he otherwise looked happy and healthy. Charles was my patient, although now that his kidney disease was in remission, I saw him only once a year for relatively quick and uneventful visits. We spent most of our sessions talking about his family and his job with the city's sanitation department. He told me he sometimes was assigned to street sweeping the area around the hospital, but this was only the second time I'd ever seen him in the midst of working. We both seemed excited about this chance encounter outside the clinic setting.

One of the parenting books suggested to me by a family therapist promoted a parenting philosophy guided by the phrase "I see you." This mantra applied in both a literal and a metaphorical sense. "I see you teasing your brother," for example. Or, in better times, "I see you encouraging your brother to play Legos with you. What a great big sister thing to do!" But "I see you" was meant to be much more than just a way to call out a child on her missteps or recognize good behavior. I see you for who you are, parents should be communicating at all times. I am observing you because I'm curious about you. I want to learn about you and be excited about the same things you're excited about. Parents should know their children's favorite movies, books, breakfasts, desserts, toys, songs, colors, and stuffed animals. They should be able to recite the names of their children's best friends this week and last week.[1]

This parent-as-anthropologist metaphor argues that if we observe our children long enough, we can understand their actions. In turn, if we need to correct any of these actions, we can intervene from a place of empathy rather than judgment. When I teach medical students to take a history, I coach them to maintain eye contact with patients at all times. Look between their eyebrows, I advise, if looking directly into their eyes is too difficult. The patients won't be able to tell the difference. Patients often look down or to the side when they tell their stories, but when they take the opportunity to look at their doctors, their doctors better be looking right back at them. "I see you," we want to communicate to those patients.

The best doctor-patient relationships transcend effective history taking and get to a place where the patients feel their doctors know something more about them than just their list of diseases and medications. Charles was proud of his job and happy that I ran into him at work. I saw him and something close to his true self. The next time he came into my clinic we'd both remember this morning, him inside the street sweeper and me waving to him with my goofy thumbs-up gesture from down below. I'd eventually comment on his weight gain and recommend that he lose fifteen to twenty pounds, and the mere act of my seeing him at his job increased the likelihood that he would take my suggestion as friendly and well-intentioned rather than dismiss it as another rebuke from another doctor.

Was this a parenting technique helping me as a physician, or could I spin this as a physician's technique helping me as a parent? An internist I shadowed as a medical student always put one or two personal sentences about his patients in his notes; he suggested I do the same when I had my own practice. For example, "He just returned from a skiing trip to Montana," or "Her twin granddaughters are now six and reading chapter books," or "He is thinking about moving to Virginia to be closer to his parents; his bank has a branch there so the move would be relatively easy." The internist demonstrated how these signposts in his previous notes gave him something to bring up at a patient's next visit, an illusion that he really knew his patients and even thought about them when they weren't sitting in his office. "Last time you said you might be moving to Virginia—is that still in the works?" He was treading some line between the art and artifice of medicine, but it was incredibly effective, and I've used this technique faithfully for all of my subsequent clinic patients. I see you, I know you, I care about you. I was communicating these messages to my patients but apparently not to my children.

My hospital—in fact, my entire university—recently announced a new research mission: personalized medicine. The other term for this is precision medicine. Regardless of terminology, the goal is clear. Using advances in DNA sequencing, we can potentially run a patient's entire genome in a few days at less than $2,000. By comparison, the same effort a decade earlier took years and cost about $3 billion. This rapid sequencing might eventually enable doctors to diagnose mysterious illnesses, map out a detailed disease course at the time of diagnosis, and identify the therapies that could alter this disease course on an individual basis.[2] The hospital encouraged all its doctors to promote this new mission via a dark blue pin on our white coats prompting patients to "Ask me about personalized medicine." We were also encouraged, in answering that question, to invite patients to enroll in one of our genetics research studies.

A medical school professor once refused to answer a question my classmate posed because she began with the word, "Why." "*Why* questions are meant for philosophers and religious scholars," this professor said. "Doctors should only try to answer *how* questions." His response seemed cheeky then (circa 2000) and today would sound antiquated. Nearly every major university hospital in this country launched its own version of a precision medicine program to match (and receive funding from) the $215 million Precision Medicine Initiative announced by President Obama in his 2015 State of the Union Address. These programs and this initiative are built upon the idea that *why* questions in medicine should indeed be asked and, when answered, will provide (as the White House press release touts) "a new model of patient-powered research that promises to accelerate biomedical discoveries and provide clinicians with new tools, knowledge, and therapies to select which treatments will work best for which patients."[3]

I think it's important for doctors to ask—and try to answer—why questions, because these are the questions our patients are asking. Genome sequencing technology is currently the best chance I have at answering the question that nearly every patient poses to me at their first appointment: "Why did this happen to me?" And the information that comes out of trying to answer this question with precision medicine might, in turn, provide the answer to this same patient's next question: "How can you make me better?" I also think that kids, especially when in turmoil, are asking these same two questions to their parents over and over and over again.

The best doctor I've ever known at making patients feel better was James Bryan, an internist who was in his eighties when I was a resident in North Carolina. Dr. Bryan occasionally precepted in residents' clinic, but I learned the most by watching him visit his patients in the hospital. He'd arrive early in the morning and limp over to the nursing station, resting his cane against a chair. "How's my friend doing?" he'd asked one of the nurses, who somehow knew exactly which patient he was referring to and summarily relayed the report from overnight. "If you need me," Dr. Bryan would say, to the air, to whichever doctors or nurses were in the vicinity, "I'll be cutting toenails." And off he ambled to the patient's room. This wasn't just a North Carolina idiom. He carried a nail clipper in his white coat pocket, and he sat by his patients' beds and talked to them while carefully clipping their nails.

Twenty or thirty minutes later, he'd sidle up next to the intern or resident taking care of his patient, place his wrinkled but still strong hands on the young doctor's shoulder, and relay a treatment plan in his charming, Southern way. "I don't think Ms. Thompson needs all those antibiotics," he might say. "Why don't you just whittle it down to one, the amoxicillin, and then send her out tomorrow." Or, "I know, just like you know, that Mr. Smith has a bleeding ulcer, but he doesn't want another endoscopy. Tell the GI guys they can call off the dogs." Or, "Have you considered checking a sedimentation rate on Mrs. Granger? I have a feeling she has temporal arteritis." And he was always right.

At the time, I considered Dr. Bryan a diagnostic genius, a real-life version of Dr. House without the ego or the bravado or the antisocial personality, just the cane and the limp. Six decades of doctoring had drafted a medical encyclopedia into his brain, to which he still had full access. Now that I have my own patients and pay the kind of "social visits" in the hospital that Dr. Bryan did (sans nail clipper, I must admit), I recognize that Dr. Bryan's genius extended well beyond basic diagnostics. His encyclopedic knowledge wasn't just about antibiotics or rheumatologic conditions but also extended to his patients. He knew them like old friends. He saw them as more than patients and took the time to learn about their families, jobs, hobbies, fears, and expectations. He listened to them in his office, on the phone, and while clipping their toenails in hospital rooms, and then he made his recommendations influenced by what they told him.

I am proudest of my own doctoring when I feel myself following Dr. Bryan's example of personalized medicine. I can never be as magnanimous and kindhearted with my patients as Dr. Bryan was with his. It just isn't in my nature. I can't call a patient "friend" without some hint of irony. But I can strive to have the same respect for my patients as he had with his, a respect born of taking the time to know them beyond just their ailments and pill bottles. Xenia was referring to this kind of respect when she asked me why I was treating my patients better than my children. This kind of respect underlies the "I see you" approach in any relationship, be it doctor and patient or parent and child.

"Precision parenting" may be an answer for the many moms and dads who are feeling the same kinds of pressures and managing the same lofty expectations as modern physicians. Being a parent, like being a doctor, is supposed to be a noble calling. When our performances fall short of whatever standards we have for these roles, the failure is compounded by the knowledge that we've affected a vulnerable population. I feel awful if I miss a diagnosis, just like I feel awful if I yell at one of my children. If a chef messes up an order, a lawyer botches a contract, or an advertiser's last commercial didn't exactly land with viewers, I'm sure they all feel bad about their missteps, but the stakes are not the same as when a doctor fails. I recognize there are plenty of other professions that impact human lives on a daily basis—teachers, police officers, and firefighters quickly come to mind— but the expectations appear to be highest for doctors. Doctors with children transfer these same expectations on themselves when it comes to parenting, as Xenia and I do, but I don't think we're exceptional or alone in this respect. I think every parent recognizes how high the stakes are in raising their children.

The precision medicine movement appeals to physicians because it promises the hope of better job performance in the form of more information, but this improved performance will only be afforded to those doctors who know how to use this information. Parents today have nearly unlimited and immediate access—via books, podcasts, websites, and social media threads—to a trove of information on how to raise their children, but, like physicians, their performance rests entirely on how this information is utilized. Precision parenting, as I see it, allows moms and dads to modify parenting to their and their children's needs by combining elements of professional advice with more commonsense and individualized tactics. The same template holds for personalized medicine: a doctor with a detailed DNA readout is not able to help her patient unless she can understand what these results mean for this specific patient, devise a treatment plan based on these results, and ultimately convince the patient to follow this treatment plan. Some of these steps rely on medical expertise and professional knowledge, while others rely on trust building and effective communication that cannot be simulated.

Precision parenting, like precision medicine, may tout a future that is unattainable—we can't cure everyone and we can't all raise perfect children—but the optimism behind these movements is important for the psyche of doctors and parents alike. Indeed, I do not intend this analogy between parenting and doctoring to be a way of ignoring the emotions involved between parents and their children. Instead, I hope this analogy shows the common dilemma that highly engaged doctors and parents both experience: how to perform an increasingly difficult job at a very high level without suffering from burnout. The answer to this dilemma is finding the joy in the process. Precision medicine begins with genotyping a patient—unraveling their genetic code—but can only function with effective *phenotyping*—constructing the most detailed observation of an individual's characteristics—of the same patient. And it's this phenotyping that provides the joy, the wonder, the "job satisfaction" for physicians and parents. For moms and dads, this phenotyping is the only way to tailor their parenting efforts toward an achievable and successful goal for each individual child.

Xenia texted me a video to cheer me up on a recent Saturday morning when I was working a weekend shift. "Our little bookworm," she captioned the video, which showed Joaquin sitting at his bookshelf, surrounded by a pile of board books. He quickly flipped through the pages of the book in his hand, threw it into the pile, and pulled another book off the shelf. "So cute," I texted back, "but also so creepy. We have the exact same video with Juno on the iPad." Later that night, I watched the video of Juno, taken six years earlier. The camera on Xenia's current iPhone shot a much crisper video than the iPad's now ancient hardware, but otherwise the two videos were almost perfect matches. Same room, same bookshelf, probably the same books. Joaquin's face was a replica of Juno's infant face, and he moved like her, squealed like her, smiled like her.

Mateo's infancy never reminded me of Juno's in this way. He didn't look at all like her. He was far more mobile than she was—crawling by seven months, walking by nine months—and would have never sat still at a bookshelf like his older sister or younger brother. He didn't really take to books at all, in fact, and was much happier to play with musical instruments or blocks or trucks, anything that allowed him to produce loud sounds. His disposition, too, was different early on compared to Juno's. He could be grouchy. He didn't smile or laugh on demand. He got labeled colicky by virtually every adult who tried to hold him. Some of this, we eventually learned, was due to food allergies, and his irritability did subside once Xenia cut dairy, soy, and eggs from her diet. But even on a restricted diet, he was "spirited," as some of the parenting books would say.

That spiritedness persisted through infancy and now into the toddler years. I suspected it would be a defining trait for him throughout the rest of his childhood. The more time I spent trying to understand his perspective, trying to see the world through his eyes, the more I realized the positives of his unique personality. Yes, I still wished I could send him to his room with orders to read for thirty minutes while I enjoyed a cup of coffee and some quiet time with a book, which is something I have always been able to do with Juno and suspect I will be able to do with Joaquin. But only Mateo could regale me with an hour-long performance in the living room, playing his toy guitar and using the wooden stand for his child-size broom, mop, and dustpan as a makeshift microphone. I learned to love the almost violent way he brushed his teeth and acquiesced to his requests for harder and harder bear hugs when I said goodbye to him at school. When I prepared snacks for him, I rolled each berry between my fingers to judge its consistency, popping the softer ones into my own mouth so that he could get his ideal fruit platter of "no squishies." And then I watched, with pleasure, how he ate with a smile splayed across his face.

The modern version of personalized medicine, rooted in rapid genome sequencing, is expected to increase a doctor's efficiency. We no longer will have to spend visit after visit unraveling our patients' histories, looking for subtle changes in their exams, serially following their laboratory values and imaging studies. A genome readout will potentially trump all of these data. This efficiency, however, may come at the expense of the old-fashioned version of personalized medicine, the James Bryan version, the version I was already employing with my patients at work and now trying to do with my children at home.

Empathy rather than solutions. I kept coming back to that phrase, how easily it could be applied to both doctoring and parenting. Personalized or precision medicine, the brand advertised by the pin on my white coat, focused entirely on solutions. Conversely, how could a doctor be more empathic than sitting at the bedside of a sick patient, clipping toenails and listening to whatever the patient wanted to share? These two versions of doctoring didn't have to be mutually exclusive. I could do both: provide empathy and then offer solutions. My patients wanted me to listen to them but also to help them. I did too. I became a doctor not just to care but also to heal.

And if I could do both empathy and solutions as a doctor, I should be able to do both as a father. On my Notes app, I kept a running diary of phrases and lines of dialogue from all the parenting books I'd been reading, a reference I could turn to whenever I needed a quick refresher to get out of a parenting crisis. I couldn't recall which book had suggested "empathy rather than solutions," but I nonetheless edited the entry, replacing "rather than" with "before." *Empathy before solutions*. The solutions part of parenting came naturally to me, whether it was helping Juno with her math homework, guiding Mateo up a rock climbing wall, or eliciting laughs from Joaquin by rubbing my stubbly chin against his belly. I became a father because of these kinds of solutions, because I wanted to spend my days and nights making my children's lives better. I didn't have to give up those goals, just place them after the simpler task of ensuring my children knew I was always available to clip their toenails.[4]

Mateo called out music requests from his car seat while Joaquin sat quietly in his infant seat, sucking on a teething toy. We'd just dropped off Juno at her bus stop and now, with her out of the car, Mateo was emboldened to ask for his desired songs. When she was in the car, he'd only ask for "Juno's playlist," a Spotify collection of forty-plus songs that Juno had assembled with my help. Her choices were mostly strong: beside the usual six-year-old fare of popular hits from the *Sing* and *Trolls* movie soundtracks, she had included songs from Van Halen, Hinds, Arcade Fire, Frank Ocean, Taylor Swift, and the Silver Jews. Her first-grade friends didn't know any of these songs, I surmised, unless they had fathers with identical music tastes as mine. Today was her last day of school. Less than two years ago, she'd been afraid to board the bus to kindergarten, and now she marched triumphantly up the bus's stairs and high-fived its driver, Mr. Sonny. "I'm not going to see you again until you're in second grade," I'd said to her before she boarded the bus, our inside joke about how fast school designations can change. She'd left the house a first grader and would come home a second grader.

"Play 'Du Toto,'" Mateo said. "I want 'Du Toto.'" I advanced through the songs on his Spotify playlist until finding Mark Ronson's "Uptown Funk." Mateo's name for the song sprang from its bass line. Most kids, if they didn't know the name for this song, would have landed on a name based on its Bruno Mars lyrics. Juno, for example, sometimes referred to it as "Don't believe me, just watch." Mateo's identification with its bass line, rather than its lyrics, reflected (I hoped) the burgeoning musician inside him. "Du," he now sang, "Du Toto, Du Toto. Du. Du Toto, Du Toto." He reached over and grabbed Joaquin's hand to try to enlist him in this musical moment.

I sang along, truly enamored by the tune after weeks of listening to it whenever we were in the car. There's an irrational love that develops for a song you associate with your children: at some point during the fiftieth or hundredth listen, the song takes on new meaning and complexity. A background vocal, a guitar riff, a one-second pause—some feature emerges that marks this song as genius, purely because you've listened to it so many times, under so many different circumstances, amid cheers and crying and even the occasional silence, and now you feel like you know every last detail of the song just like you know every last detail of your child.

This week was "Uptown Funk." The previous week, though, I'd had the same experience with Katy Perry's "Roar," proclaiming it (in my own head, of course, never out loud to any other adult) the most underrated pop song of the last decade. I could have done an extended monologue on the intricacies of Katy Perry's music the way Patrick Bateman waxed poetic about Huey Lewis in *American Psycho*. The staccato introduction of "Roar" lulls the listener into thinking this will be another sweet Katy Perry tune, with a pretty vocal and saccharine message. She begins singing in a soft and non-confrontational voice about how meek she used to be. Quiet. Conforming. The good girl everyone expected. As we march toward the chorus, it's the music that first becomes louder and more aggressive. We hear a pounding bass drum and the introduction of an electric guitar best described as raw and crunchy. Suddenly we're in the chorus, with Katy singing loudly and confidently about how strong she can be, followed by a series of notes from the back of her throat that evoke a yodel and show no signs of self-consciousness. She seems to be channeling Dolores O'Riordan, the late singer of the Cranberries, and her guttural yelps in their 1994 classic, "Zombie." This is not a stretch. Later in the song, when Katy approaches the chorus with a crescendo-ing bridge of "Roar! Roar! Roar!," she is a dead ringer for O'Riordan's shouts in "Zombie."

Patrick Bateman was a sociopath, though. His hyper-intellectual approach to the tepid catalogue of Huey Lewis was one of the more humorous aspects of *American Psycho*, a way for its author to show Bateman's delusion and distance from reality while still having a bit of a joke at the expense of Huey Lewis and his fans. Was my infatuation with Katy Perry the previous week, and now with Mark Ronson and "Du Toto," a sign that I was losing my own grip on reality? Yes. The answer was yes. Being a totally invested parent meant being a little bit crazy. Xenia had once claimed that the kids had Stockholm syndrome with me. Well, I had Stockholm syndrome with the songs on their playlists but also with my captors themselves, Juno and Mateo and Joaquin. As we pulled into the day care, I reveled in the secret language Mateo and I shared. Other than me, no one else in the world—not his mother, not his day care teacher, not even Mark Ronson himself—would be able to hear him ask for "Du Toto" and immediately know he wanted "Uptown Funk." We shared a good kind of crazy.

After work, when I picked Mateo up, his day care teacher said, almost sheepishly, that she had some forms for me. I knew what this meant. "Forms" was shorthand for incident reports, the triplicate sheets that day care teachers were required to fill out when a child was injured in any way. "Uh-oh," I said. Then, in a whisper, I asked, "Did he bite someone?" He hadn't bitten anyone in months, the result, I hoped, of concentrated efforts to help him modulate his anger. Getting an incident report now felt like receiving a failing grade on a surprise quiz.

"No biting," his teacher said. "He tried to grab a toy from one of his friends, and the friend scratched him behind his ear."

"Oh," I said. "And he didn't do anything back?"

"He told us," the teacher said. "The scratch is still there."

"I guess that's good," I said, not to the teacher but more to myself. "It's good he didn't hit back in any way."

At that point, Mateo ran over to me and hugged my leg. "Jacob scratched me," he said excitedly, pulling back his ear lobe to show me his battle wounds. His teacher, as per protocol, had deliberately omitted the other combatant's name, but Mateo was not obliged to respect such confidentiality rules. I dropped to my knees. "Ouch," I said. "That must have hurt. You must have felt sad that Jacob did that. And I bet Jacob felt sad he did that too."

Mateo nodded and put on a sad face that had to be deliberate, given how happily he'd just relayed the incident with Jacob. I knew his teacher was listening to me. In a way, I was showing off some of the verbiage I'd learned from all the parenting books I'd read over the last few months. I was helping Mateo take control of his emotions. This forced expression of sadness on his face, just like his finding a teacher to defuse a fight, should be considered a success.

"Maybe tomorrow you can tell Jacob you're sorry for trying to take the toy away from him, but you also felt hurt when he scratched you. I'm sure Jacob will say he's sorry too."

"He will?" Mateo asked.

"He will," I said.

We picked up Joaquin from the infant room and headed out to the car. Once we were on the road, ritually listening to "Du Toto," I chewed over the incident report. Why wasn't I happier about the scratching skirmish and Mateo's controlled response? He'd done exactly what the books had promised he could do if he worked on anger management and emotion modulation. But had we reprogrammed something natural out of him in the process? I looked at his reflection in the rearview mirror. He wasn't enjoying "Du Toto" as much as he usually did. In fact, he hadn't even asked for the song. I'd just reflexively started playing it once I started the car. Perhaps his sadness wasn't feigned. His body and his feelings had been hurt.

I sang along, extra loud, to snap Mateo out of whatever funk he'd fallen into at the end of his day. "Du!" I chanted. "Du Toto! Du Toto!"

"Stop it, Daddy," he whined from his seat. When I kept on singing, just as loudly, he screamed the request.

"Okay," I said, turning off the car stereo. I could hear Mateo sucking loudly on his shirt collar. "How's Joaquin doing back there?" I asked.

"He's okay," Mateo said. "He's playing with his lovie."

"And how's Mateo?" When he didn't answer, I said, "You seem sad."

"A little. Also tired. And hungry."

"Well, we're almost home. Then we can eat dinner and get ready for bed and read your favorite books and then get some sleep. Sound good?"

"Yes," he said. And then, a moment later, he said, "Daddy?"

"Yes."

"Can you put 'Du Toto' back on?"

"Of course."

I blasted "Uptown Funk" and sang along with him to the final chorus. "Uptown funk you up, uptown funk you up!" we yelled. And then, because it was a beautiful day, I turned off the air conditioner, rolled down the windows, and opened up the sunroof, too, so that Mateo couldn't make out what I was singing. While he chirped away from his car seat, from my own seat I shifted into the lyrics that I knew Juno sang whenever she allowed him to play the song in the car. "Uptown fuck you up, uptown fuck you up!" I sang. "Uptown fuck you up, uptown fuck you up!" I watched Mateo in the rearview mirror, waiting for him to lock eyes with me.

"I see you, Daddy," he said.

"I see you too."

Epilogue: Parenting during a Pandemic

When the next pandemic hits, I'm going to immediately remove every reminder about my children's extracurricular activities from my phone. I finally did this about ten weeks into the COVID-19 pandemic, and the relief was palpable. I no longer got a vibrating buzz every hour with a five-minute warning about a violin lesson, gymnastics class, Girl Scout meeting, swim session, or soccer practice that had, by then, been canceled indefinitely. These calendar prompts were constant reminders not only of all the opportunities my children were missing due to the pandemic but also of all the unstructured time now left for me and my wife to fill on our own. Before the pandemic, when Xenia and I were shuttling the five-year-old from soccer to violin, and the eight-year-old from violin to Scouts, and somehow trying to figure out if we could squeeze in a friend's birthday party for the two-year-old, we appreciated how the phone's calendar and its reminders kept us on track. Now, they were regularly scheduled taunts—you overschedule your kids, you rely on others to take

care of them, you have removed spontaneity and flex-
ibility from their lives—that I eventually decided were
unnecessary.

I was watching my children play in a dirty stream
when I erased every parenting reminder from my calendar. My phone buzzed to inform me that Juno's violin
lesson was about to begin; in thirty minutes, I'd be getting another buzz for Mateo's lesson. I watched as they
tried to build a dam out of rocks and encouraged their
younger brother, Joaquin, to join their fun with the few
pebbles he could carry in his tiny hands. Violin lessons
were a thing of a not-too-distant past that felt, at that
moment, very distant.

The morning had been a success in spite of, or more
likely because of, all my plans falling by the wayside. I
wanted to give Xenia a quiet house so that she could
sleep in for a change, so I loaded the kids into the car
with promises of muffins from the local coffee shop and
an outdoor snack in the lone playground our town had
not roped off due to COVID restrictions. "Can we bring
our rain boots so we can play in the stream?" Juno asked.
I told her no, I didn't want to deal with the cleanup,
but she promised she'd get her younger brothers to
bathe when we returned home. I gave in and threw
their boots in the trunk. When we arrived at the coffee shop, the social distancing-compliant line stretched
down the block. I had three kids—eight, five, and two—
and an estimated wait time of thirty minutes. "Plan B,"
I announced to my charges. "We're going to Dunkin'

Donuts instead." The kids cheered while the adults on line passed their judgments on me for not teaching my children patience and opting for processed, chain-brand, sugar cakes rather than supporting a local business and giving my children homemade, farm-to-table pastries. Or so it seemed. But an hour later, my kids' bellies were full of Munchkins, and they were splashing around in a filthy stream, laughing through mud-splattered smiles.

When I deleted the violin lessons and all the other weekly reminders that offered nothing during a pandemic, the phone repeatedly asked if I wanted to delete just this one occurrence or "all future events." Are you sure you're ready to commit to this, the phone seemed to be asking, and that morning, the answer was a resounding yes. I have heard similar epiphany-like moments from other moms and dads about parenting during COVID-19 times, when they suddenly realized the unique opportunity this pandemic provided their family. "There's something nice about having a day with absolutely nothing to do, nowhere to go, and no one to see other than your kids," one mother told me. "Of course, day after day after day of that becomes a major challenge, but I can't remember the last time we had a completely open weekend like the ones we're having now. Even when we were on quote-unquote vacation, we followed a schedule, but not now. And the kids seem to like it. Hopefully when things open back up, we'll learn something from this, loosen things up for them."

My own mother said something similar to me later that day when we spoke on the phone. Joaquin was home napping, and I'd taken the older kids to their elementary school to ride bikes in the parking lot. A few other families had the same idea, so as the parents stood off to the side, we periodically pulled down our masks to remind our children to keep a safe distance from the other children. This was a bit of performance art. We all likely felt somewhat guilty about the group gathering, even if it was not planned, so we needed to signal that we were being as responsible as possible in this setting. The kids needed to get out of their homes. We needed them to entertain themselves so we could read a book or scroll Twitter or, in my case, speak to my parents without distractions.

"I think kids are going to learn something from this," my mother was saying as I watched Mateo, who was relatively new and overly confident on a two-wheeler, dip between two skateboarders. "And parents, too. You know, I always say that if I had things like indoor playgrounds and waffle cafes and trampoline parks to bring you and your brothers to, it would have made my life much easier. But really, even without those, I don't think it was as hard for me as it is for you and your brothers and your sisters-in-law. You guys played a lot on your own."

I watched as Juno took a break from her bike to grab a granola bar and her water bottle from the bag sitting on the hood of my car. I'm sure my mom packed snacks for me and my brothers, but I don't remember that being a crucial part of any time we left the house the way it is for my kids. I never had my own water bottle. I distinctly remember my mom telling my brothers and me, when we complained of being thirsty, to drink our own spit. She said it with a smile.

"We are flying the plane as we build it." Xenia is an internist but also the chief quality officer for her hospital, which was one of the first in the United States to have a patient test positive for COVID-19. In the initial weeks of the pandemic, she was up late every night on phone calls and Zoom meetings discussing how to contain the infection rate within her hospital. I heard her and her colleagues use the plane analogy over and over again.

Parents were in a comparable position of trying to manage a precarious situation without any blueprint upon which to rely. For families without food or internet access, struggling with domestic or substance abuse, the pandemic and its stay-at-home decree created another, parallel state of emergency. For moms and dads fortunate enough not to worry about such high-risk stressors, the stakes were admittedly lower compared to Xenia's hospital—how to fill the hours of the day once the thirty-minute Google classroom session has ended is, of course, no match for how to contain a potentially lethal virus. Still, the pressure to rise to this moment was similarly high for parents. Kids were stuck at home with no outside help available. Babysitters, whether they be local teenagers or grandparents, were obeying shelter-in-place orders.

"The history of parenting is, in large part, a history of trying to get out of it," according to Jennifer Traig. In *Act Natural: A Cultural History of Misadventures in Parenting*, Traig traces the history of "allo-parenting," a technical term for getting someone else to watch your kids, all the way back to the earliest humans who exposed their unwanted children to the elements.[1] Over time, parents found more humane ways to absolve themselves of child-rearing responsibilities, whether it be in the form of wet nurses, tutors, governesses, or older siblings charged with taking care of all the young ones. Childcare, as we know it, is a relatively new phenomenon, but shipping off the kids to someone else's charge has been in practice for centuries. COVID-19 abruptly erased this option.

For many families, the only form of allo-parenting available during the pandemic was its most modern iteration: television, aka the electronic babysitter. "It sucks," Casey, a mother of three (5, 7, and 12), told me when she described how much television her kids were now watching. "But if I couldn't put them in front of the TV for an hour here or an hour there, there's no way I could do my own work, sneak in exercise, or even talk to you without interruption." I'd asked her to speak with me over Zoom about her parenting experiences during the pandemic in part because she was a middle-school teacher and in part because, during the first few weeks of stay-at-home orders, she posted daily Facebook updates on her attempts to educate, entertain, and support her kids during these unprecedented times. "And then throw in the fact that their school is now basically a computer, so it's even more of them just sitting in front of a screen all day."

Casey's Facebook posts highlighted her unique style of creative, do-it-yourself lessons for her children, all of which were designed to get the kids away from screens and thinking on their own. For "music class," she played them a variety of songs (classical, country, folk, hip-hop, pop, jazz), asked them to choose their favorite, and then write about why they'd chosen that song. Experiments with ingredients from the refrigerator and pantry served as science class. Her kids drew maps and made collages about faraway countries for social studies. And each day included some form of outdoor exercise in lieu of gym class, whether it was jumping jacks in the backyard or taking a walk in full rain gear during a storm. As the Facebook posts were the only glimpse I'd had into her pandemic life, I was surprised (and admittedly relieved) to hear her lament about how much television she was allowing her kids these days.

"I was showing the successes," she said, "mostly because I was really proud of how well we were handling this." Because she still had to maintain her full teaching responsibilities, Casey would schedule two-hour blocks for her own students, followed by two-hour blocks for her children. The two-hour blocks in which she was fully engaged with her students, while her kids were in another part of the house, posed a new challenge. Early on in the pandemic, her mother made the decision to enter their bubble. "That's been a huge help," Casey said. "But even she needs a break once in a while, so, yeah, back to the TV."

When I spoke with Casey, the school year had just ended, and she hadn't posted anything on Facebook in weeks. I was surprised to learn why she'd stopped sharing her home schooling experiences. I assumed the successes had dried up, that the plane she'd been building and flying at the same time had crashed back to the reality that "good parenting" was impossible during the pandemic, especially with small children like ours. As humor writer Kimberly Harrington tweeted, "Based on my current experience, the only parenting advice I have to give you is you should've had your kids 2003–2007ish."[2] Tales of parental woes—exemplified by essays like Chloe Cooney's "The Parents Are Not All Right"[3] and Farhad Manjoo's "Two Parents. Two Kids. Two Jobs. No Child Care,"[4] as well as a series of New York Times reader comments curated under the title "I Have Given Up: Parenting in Quarantine"[5]—appeared everywhere to provide parents like me with a little bit of solace that our kids weren't the only ones leading a life of junk food, flexible bedtimes, and hours in front of a screen that would have never been permitted during normal times.

"I got some negative feedback," Casey told me. "Some moms contacted me and asked me to stop posting because I was making them feel bad." Her Facebook posts routinely elicited public comments of gratitude and appreciation—"Love this idea! Going to try this tomorrow!"—but the private messages she received were the exact opposite. The directionality of parent shaming in this instance was complicated. Other parents were criticizing Casey for making pandemic parenting look easy. They saw her posts as a rebuke of their own failed attempts at getting their kids to learn and exercise and smile while stuck at home. Their response to this perceived parent shaming was to shame right back. Tell the truth, they demanded of her, and admit that this sucks and you're just in denial.

With a select group of other mothers, Casey formed a private group on the Marco Polo app, sending and receiving quick videos that became a running conversation on the frustrations of parenting during the pandemic. I asked her to describe the exchanges. "You know, things like, 'I sounded just like my mother when I yelled at my kids' or 'My kid tried to actually eat this thing.' It's mostly a space to just vent and listen to someone else venting." These confessions—both the ones she sent and the ones she received from her friends—were cathartic for her. "You know, we're all struggling with the same things," she said. But her Facebook posts were intended to be different, an optimistic message to other parents that this time didn't have to be awful and could have some silver linings. "But it was upsetting people," she conceded, "so I stopped."

Although COVID-19 posed a once-in-a-lifetime challenge to people all across the world, the issues with which moms and dads struggled were not necessarily unique to the pandemic. Rather, the abrupt changes brought about by school and day care closures, stay-at-home orders, and social distancing guidelines accelerated and magnified the same problems that have made parenting so difficult ever since "parent" changed from a noun to a verb. Spending more time with their children heightened expectations for parents and exaggerated failures when these (likely unrealistic) expectations could not be met.

Xenia and I often complained, prior to the pandemic, that parenting would be easier and more productive if we simply had more time with our kids, if we didn't have to get everything right in a short period of time that progressively shrank with every demand from our jobs, every violin lesson or swim class, every play date or birthday party. The pandemic granted that opportunity, and yet parenting became harder for most mothers and fathers. That is why I eventually removed all those calendar reminders from my phone. They were not just reminders of activities my kids could no longer enjoy, but also reminders of how much I needed to outsource my parenting responsibilities to make fatherhood manageable.

The struggles of modern parenting are a reflection more of the adults than of the kids. This rang even truer during the pandemic. Dr. Kelly Fradin, a pediatrician and mother of two, emphasizes the importance of parental self-care in her book, *Parenting in a Pandemic: How to Help Your Family Through COVID-19*.[6] Parents set the tone for children, Fradin notes, and parental martyrdom bears consequences, including the contagion of anxiety and depression. In an editorial for the *New York Times* entitled "Who Can Endure the Loneliness of This Moment?," Michelle Goldberg divulged her own feelings of seclusion, boredom, frustration, and joylessness, and explored how this kind of confession was taboo in certain circles. "It's easier to discuss what it's doing to our kids," Goldberg wrote, "because we feel justified in trying to spare them pain."[7] And on January 1, 2021, a tweet from Matthew Segal, a civil rights lawyer, went viral: "I think children deserve a ton of credit for how they handled 2020. We asked them to change their lives in terrible ways largely for the protection of adults. And they did it."[8] The tens of thousands of retweets Segal earned suggests, to me, that his missive provided a bit of parent shaming for the Twitterverse.

So much of modern parenting is performance. Performance in making your kids think you enjoy reading *Elmo's Fuzzy Valentine* twenty nights in a row. Performance in not telling other parents that you secretly fantasize about hiding *Elmo's Fuzzy Valentine* in this week's recycling. Performance in never letting anyone, save for perhaps your partner, your therapist, or, in Casey's case, a select group of friends on a confidential video sharing app, know that the job often sucks. A pandemic doesn't change this need for performance. It only makes the performance harder.

Even in good—or, at least we can say, normal—times, the role of mother or father remains a mystery (why is my son dipping his scrambled eggs into milk?), a challenge (how can I prevent my daughter from waking up at 2:30 a.m. every single night?), or an insurmountable feat (will these kids ever stop teasing each other?). The seemingly endless supply of parenting tools—books, websites, podcasts, support groups—claim to make these roles easier by, in essence, acknowledging that parents are indeed on stage and providing a script for the actors to follow. But as someone who's consumed far too many of these well-intentioned sources, I've always felt that the script is intended for a play that takes place at someone else's house, and I suspect most parents have felt that way at times. In other words, from day one, parenting can feel like a version of "we are flying the plane as we build it," with or without a pandemic.

At the end of my conversation with Casey, I asked her what she had planned for her kids during the summer. Camps, like schools, were closed, so she was staring at three months of having to entertain the kids on her own. "But at least they won't have to compete with my work," she said. "It should be easier just focusing on them." She asked how Xenia and I were tackling the summer months.

"We're each taking a week and a half of vacation time to watch them," I said, "so that covers us for three weeks, and then we'll just have to hire a babysitter to watch them for the other seven weeks."

"Wow," Casey said. "Seven weeks of having someone else watch my kids sounds amazing right now."

Acknowledgments

Thank you to Matt McGowan for championing this book from its earliest stages. Thank you to Matt Browne, Kathleen Caruso, Susan Clark, Anne-Marie Bono, and their colleagues at the MIT Press for guiding this book to its current form.

Thank you to Janine Annett, Jared Beasley, Mark Bomback, Chloe Caldwell, Nancy Dodson, Sean Hastings, and Dorothy Neagle for reading sections of this book (before it was a book) and giving me incredibly useful feedback.

Thank you to Michele Pridmore-Brown (*Los Angeles Review of Books*), Lydia Kiesling (*The Millions*), and Aaron Burch (*Hobart*) for publishing portions of this book (again, before it was a book).

Thank you to Xenia, Ariadne, Juno, Mateo, and Joaquin for EVERYTHING!

Notes

Author's Note

1. Frank Faranda, *The Fear Paradox: How Our Obsession with Feeling Secure Imprisons Our Minds and Shapes Our Lives* (Coral Gables, FL: Mango Publishing Group, 2020).

2. Andrew Bomback, *Doctor* (New York: Bloomsbury Academic, 2019).

3. Jennifer Traig, *Act Natural: A Cultural History of Misadventures in Parenting* (New York: Ecco, 2019).

4. Paula S. Fass, *The End of American Childhood: A History of Parenting from Life on the Frontier to the Managed Child* (Princeton, NJ: Princeton University Press, 2016).

5. Joseph Henrich, *The WEIRDest People in the World: How the West Became Psychologically Peculiar and Particularly Prosperous* (New York: Farrar, Straus and Giroux, 2020).

6. Gretchen Rubin, *The Happiness Project: Or, Why I Spent a Year Trying to Sing in the Morning, Clean My Closets, Fight Right, Read Aristotle, and Generally Have More Fun* (New York: HarperCollins, 2009).

7. Ada Calhoun, *Why We Can't Sleep: Women's New Midlife Crisis* (New York: Grove Press, 2020).

Chapter 1

1. Atul Gawande, "Curiosity and What Equality Really Means," *New Yorker*, June 2, 2018.

2. Beth Ann Fennelly, *Heating & Cooling: 52 Micro-Memoirs* (New York: W. W. Norton, 2018).

Chapter 2

1. Chimamanda Ngozi Adichie, *Dear Ijeawele, or A Feminist Manifesto in Fifteen Suggestions* (New York: Anchor, 2017).

2. Claire Cain Miller, "The Relentlessness of Modern Parenting," *New York Times*, December 25, 2018.

3. The Google Books Ngram for "parenting" can be accessed at https://books.google.com/ngrams/graph?content=parenting &corpus=15&direct_url=t1%3B,parenting%3B,c0&share=&smoothing =3&year_end=2008&year_start=1900.

4. Fitzhugh Dodson, *How to Parent* (Chicago, IL: Nash Publishing, 1970). Dodson went on to write *How to Father* (1975), *How to Grandparent* (1984), and *How to Single Parent* (1988), but he never recaptured the success of his original book.

5. Jennifer Senior, *All Joy and No Fun: The Paradox of Modern Parenthood* (New York: Ecco, 2014).

6. Peter N. Stearns, *Anxious Parents: A History of Modern Childrearing in America* (New York: New York University Press, 2003).

7. Kim Brooks, *Small Animals: Parenthood in the Age of Fear* (New York: Flatiron Books, 2018). In the author's own words, "The object of fear correlates less to the level of risk than to parents' ability (or perceived ability) to exert control over the outcome."

8. Nora Ephron, *I Feel Bad about My Neck: And Other Thoughts on Being a Woman* (New York: Knopf Doubleday, 2006).

9. Jennifer Glass, Robin W. Simon, and Matthew A. Anderson, "Parenthood and Happiness: Effects of Work-Family Reconciliation

Policies in 22 OECD Countries," *American Journal of Sociology* 122, no. 3 (2016): 886–929.

10. Paula S. Fass, *The End of American Childhood: A History of Parenting from Life on the Frontier to the Managed Child* (Princeton, NJ: Princeton University Press, 2016).

11. Ada Calhoun, *Why We Can't Sleep: Women's New Midlife Crisis* (New York: Grove Press, 2020).

Chapter 3

1. Adele Faber and Elaine Mazlish, *How to Talk So Kids Will Listen & Listen So Kids Will Talk* (New York: Simon & Schuster, 1979).

2. Joanna Faber and Julie King, *How to Talk So Little Kids Will Listen* (New York: Scribner, 2017).

3. Jennifer Traig, *Act Natural: A Cultural History of Misadventures in Parenting* (New York: Ecco, 2019).

4. Paula S. Fass, *The End of American Childhood: A History of Parenting from Life on the Frontier to the Managed Child* (Princeton, NJ: Princeton University Press, 2016).

5. Louis Starr, *Hygiene of the Nursery* (Philadelphia: P. Blakiston's Son & Co., 1888).

6. Louis Starr, *The Adolescent Period: Its Features and Management* (Philadelphia: P. Blakiston's Son & Co., 1915).

7. Benjamin Spock, *The Common Sense Book of Baby and Child Care* (New York: Pocket Books, 1946).

8. Marion LeBron, "Relax and Enjoy Your Children," *Parents' Magazine*, January 1941.

9. Heather Turgeon and Julie Wright, *Now Say This: The Right Words to Solve Every Parenting Dilemma* (New York: Tarcher Perigree, 2018).

10. Heather Turgeon and Julie Wright, *The Happy Sleeper* (New York: Tarcher Perigree, 2014).

11. Kim Brooks, *Small Animals: Parenthood in the Age of Fear* (New York: Flatiron Books, 2018).

12. Natasha Campbell and Amir Raz, "Placebo Science in Medical Education," in *Placebo Talks: Modern Perspectives on Placebos in Society*, edited by A. Raz and C. Harris (Oxford, UK: Oxford University Press, 2016).

Chapter 4

1. Bill Pratt, Mark C. Weitzel, and Len Rhodes, *How to Keep Your Kid from Moving Back Home after College* (Winterville, NC: Viaticus Publishing, 2012).

2. Jeffrey Jensen Arnett and Elizabeth Fishel, *Getting to 30: A Parent's Guide to the 20-Something Years*. (New York: Workman Publishing, 2013).

3. Claire Cain Miller, "The Relentlessness of Modern Parenting," *New York Times*, December 25, 2018.

4. William Doherty, *Take Back Your Kids: Confident Parenting in Turbulent Times* (Notre Dame, IN: Sorin Books, 2000).

5. Amy Fusselman, *Savage Park: A Meditation on Play, Space, and Risk for Americans Who Are Nervous, Distracted, and Afraid to Die* (New York: Mariner Books, 2015).

6. Paula S. Fass, *The End of American Childhood: A History of Parenting from Life on the Frontier to the Managed Child* (Princeton, NJ: Princeton University Press, 2016).

7. The Goddard School's mission statement, available at www.goddardschool.com.

8. Tasnim Nazeer, "What Is a Babymoon and Why Should You Go on One?," *Culture Trip*, November 21, 2017, https://theculturetrip.com/asia/articles/what-is-a-babymoon-and-why-should-you-go-on-one/.

9. Maria Pasquini, "What Is a Push Present—and What Kind of Gifts Do Women Typically Receive When They Get One?," *People*, February 27, 2018.

10. Mark Lino, Kevin Kuczynski, Nestor Rodriguez, and TusaRebecca Shap, *Expenditures on Children by Families, 2015*, Miscellaneous Publication No. 1528-2015, U.S. Department of Agriculture, Center for Nutrition Policy and Promotion, January 2017, https://cdn2.hubspot .net/hubfs/10700/blog-files/USDA_Expenditures%20on%20chil dren%20by%20family.pdf?t=1520090048492.

11. U.S. Bureau of Labor Statistics, *Occupational Employment and Wage Statistics*, Occupational Employment and Wages, May 2020, https://www.bls.gov/oes/current/oes399011.htm.

12. Caitlin McLean, Lea J. E. Austin, Marcy Whitebrook, and Krista L. Olson, *Early Childhood Workforce Index—2020* (Berkeley, CA: Center for the Study of Child Care Employment, University of California, Berkeley), https://cscce.berkeley.edu/workforce-index-2020/report-pdf/.

Chapter 5

1. *Louie* aired on the FX channel from 2010 to 2015, with Louis C.K. winning multiple Emmy awards for his writing on the series (which he also directed and starred in). In 2017, after years of rumors circulating about C.K.'s sexual misconduct, the *New York Times* published detailed allegations of sexual harassment against the comedian by five women with whom he'd worked. In a statement from C.K. the following day, he said, "These stories are true."

2. Karl Ove Knausgaard, *My Struggle*, trans. Don Bartlett and Martin Aitken, 6 vols. (Brooklyn, NY: Archipelago Books, 2012–2018).

3. James Wood, "Total Recall," *New Yorker*, August 13, 2012.

4. Rivka Galchen, *Little Labors* (New York: New Directions, 2016).

5. *The Bill Simmons Podcast*, originally titled *The B.S. Report* when Simmons worked for ESPN, is part of the Ringer Podcast Network.

6. Patrick A. Coleman, "What Does the Bill Simmons Podcast 'Parent Corner' Teach Dads about Parenting?," *Fatherly*, November 9, 2018.

7. Helen Phillips, *The Need* (New York: Simon & Schuster, 2019).

8. Jenny Offill, *Dept. of Speculation* (New York: Alfred A. Knopf, 2014.)

9. *Tully*, directed by Jason Reitman, written by Diablo Cody (Universal City, CA: Focus Features, 2018).

10. Leila Slimani, *The Perfect Nanny: A Novel*, trans. Sam Taylor (New York: Penguin, 2018).

11. Sara Petersen, "After the Pandemic, We'll Finally Have to Address the Impossible State of Motherhood," *In Style*, June 24, 2020.

12. Sara Petersen, "Momfluencer Content Enrages Me. Why Can't I Look Away?," *Harper's Bazaar*, January 28, 2021.

13. Sarah Vap, *Winter: Effulgences and Devotions* (Blacksburg, VA: Noemi Press, 2019).

14. Kate Chopin, *The Awakening* (Chicago, IL: H. S. Stone, 1899).

15. Jean Rhys, *Wide Sargasso Sea* (New York: W. W. Norton, 1966).

16. Susan Taubes, *Divorcing* (New York: Random House, 1969).

17. Catherine Texier, *Breakup: The End of a Love Story* (New York: Anchor Books, 1998).

18. Elena Ferrante, *The Days of Abandonment*, trans. Ann Goldstein (New York: Europa Editions, 2005) (originally published in 2002 by Edizioni e/o).

19. Julia Fine, *The Upstairs House* (New York: Harper Collins, 2021).

20. Julia Fine, *I'm a Writer But*, hosted by Alex Higley and Lindsay Hunter, June 29, 2021, podcast, https://imawriterbut.libsyn.com/julia-fine.

21. Rachel Yoder, *Nightbitch: A Novel* (New York: Doubleday, 2021).

22. Hillary Kelly, "A Novel That Imagines Motherhood as an Animal State," *New Yorker*, June 26, 2021.

23. Karen Russell, *Orange World and Other Stories* (New York: Alfred A. Knopf, 2019).

24. Tweet from Miranda July (@Miranda_July), June 2, 2018.

Chapter 6

1. US Department of Health, Education, and Welfare, Children's Bureau, *The Story of Infant Care* (Washington, DC: Children's Bureau, 1965).

2. Paula S. Fass, *The End of American Childhood: A History of Parenting from Life on the Frontier to the Managed Child* (Princeton, NJ: Princeton University Press, 2016). My discussion of *Infant Care* relies heavily on Fass's research on this book.

3. Ann Hulbert, *Raising America: Experts, Parents, and a Century of Advice about Children* (New York: Alfred A. Knopf, 2003).

4. Peter N. Stearns, *Anxious Parents: A History of Modern Childrearing in America* (New York: New York University Press, 2003).

5. Daniel J. Siegel and Tina Payne Bryson, *The Whole Brain Child: 12 Revolutionary Strategies to Nurture Your Child's Developing Mind* (New York: Delacorte Press, 2011).

6. Paul Raeburn and Kevin Zollman, *The Game Theorist's Guide to Parenting: How the Science of Strategic Thinking Can Help You Deal with the Toughest Negotiators You Know—Your Kids* (New York: Scientific American / Farrar, Straus and Giroux, 2016).

7. Emily Oster, *Cribsheet: A Data-Driven Guide to Better, More Relaxed Parenting, from Birth to Preschool* (New York: Penguin Press, 2019).

8. Emily Stimmel, "Kevin Zollman Writes 'The Game Theorist's Guide to Parenting,'" *Carnegie Mellon University News*, February 8, 2016, https://www.cmu.edu/news/stories/archives/2016/february/guide-to-parenting.html.

9. Emily Oster, *Expecting Better: Why the Conventional Pregnancy Wisdom Is Wrong—and What You Really Need to Know* (New York: Penguin Press, 2013).

10. Emily Oster, *The Family Firm: A Data-Driven Guide to Better Decision Making in the Early School Years* (New York: Penguin Press, 2021).

11. Joe Pinsker, "Parenting Like an Economist Is a Lot Less Stressful," *The Atlantic*, April 23, 2019.

12. Lewis Hyde, *The Gift: Imagination and the Erotic Life of Property* (New York: Random House, 1983).

13. Kimberly Seals Allers, "Is Data-Driven Parenting Undermining Mothers?," *The Riveter*, https://theriveter.co/voice/data-driven-parenting-kimberly-seals-allers/.

14. Philippa Perry, *The Book You Wish Your Parents Had Read (and Your Children Will Be Glad That You Did)* (London, UK: Penguin Life, 2019).

Chapter 7

1. Carol Stock Kranowitz, *The Out-of-Sync Child: Recognizing and Coping with Sensory Processing Disorder* (New York: Skylight Press, 2005).

2. Lynelle Schneeberg, *Become Your Child's Sleep Coach: The Bedtime Doctor's 5-Step Guide* (New York: Lifelong Books / Hachette Book Group, 2019).

3. Emily Paige Ballou, Sharon daVanport, and Morenike Giwa Onaiwu, eds., *Sincerely, Your Autistic Child: What People on the Autism Spectrum Wish Their Parents Knew about Growing Up, Acceptance, and Identity* (Boston, MA: Beacon Press, 2021).

4. Edward M. Hallowell and John J. Ratey, *Driven to Distraction: Recognizing and Coping with Attention Deficit Disorder* (New York: Pantheon Books, 1994).

5. Stephen P. Hinshaw and Richard M. Scheffler, *The ADHD Explosion: Myths, Medication, Money, and Today's Push for Performance* (Oxford, UK: Oxford University Press, 2014).

6. The diagnosis is listed in the *Diagnostic Classification of Mental Health and Developmental Disorders of Infancy and Early Childhood* but remains excluded from the latest edition of the *DSM* (2013) despite lobbying efforts from groups invested in the disease's classification. See *Diagnostic Classification 0–3: Diagnostic Classification of Mental Health and Developmental Disorders of Infancy and Early Childhood*, ed. Serena Wieder (Washington, DC: Zero to Three: National Center for Infants, Toddlers and Families, 1994).

7. Section On Complementary and Integrative Medicine; Council on Children with Disabilities; American Academy of Pediatrics, Michelle Zimmer, and Larry Desch, "Sensory Integration Therapies for Children with Developmental and Behavioral Disorders," *Pediatrics* 129, no. 6 (2012): 1186–1189.

8. A. Jean Ayres, "Types of Sensory Integrative Dysfunction among Disabled Learners," *American Journal of Occupational Therapy* 26, no. 1 (1972): 13–18.

9. A. Jean Ayres, *Sensory Integration and the Child: 25th Anniversary Edition* (Torrance, CA: Western Psychological Services, 2005).

10. Angie Voss, *Understanding Your Child's Sensory Signals* (Scotts Valley, CA: CreateSpace Independent Publishing Platform, 2011).

Chapter 8

1. Gary Ezzo and Robert Bucknam, *On Becoming Babywise: Giving Your Infant the Gift of Nighttime Sleep* (Sisters, OR: Parent-Wise Solutions, 1993).

2. Tracy Hogg and Melinda Blau, *Secrets of the Baby Whisperer: How to Calm, Connect, and Communicate with Your Baby* (New York: Ballantine Books, 2000).

3. Katie Allison Granju, "Getting Wise to 'Babywise,'" *Salon*, August 6, 1998. Granju's article gives a comprehensive overview of the book's origin story.

4. Matthew Aney, "'Babywise' Advice Linked to Dehydration, Failure to Thrive," *American Academy of Pediatrics News* 14, no. 4 (1998): 21.

5. Haim G. Ginott, *Between Parent and Teenager* (New York: Macmillan, 1969).

6. Gary Ezzo and Robert Bucknam, *On Becoming Babywise: Giving Your Infant the Gift of Nighttime Sleep—30th Anniversary Edition* (Sisters, OR: Hawksflight & Associates, 2020).

7. David Code, *To Raise Happy Kids, Put Your Marriage First* (Spring Valley, NY: Crossroad Publishing Company, 2009).

8. Pamela Druckerman, *Bringing Up Bébé: One American Mother Discovers the Wisdom of French Parenting* (New York: Penguin, 2012).

9. "'Bringing Up Bébé' Review: Why French Parenting Helps Kids Eat Normal Foods, Behave Themselves, and Sleep All Night," *Fatherly*, May 1, 2015.

10. Ellen Sturm Niz and Nicole Harris, "What Is Free Range Parenting, and Why Is It Controversial?," *Parents*, November 1, 2019.

11. Lenore Skenazy, "Why I Let My 9-Year-Old Ride the Subway Alone," *New York Sun*, April 1, 2008.

12. Lenore Skenazy, *Free-Range Kids: How to Raise Safe, Self-Reliant Children (Without Going Nuts with Worry)* (San Francisco, CA: Jossey-Bass, 2009).

13. Ellen Beate Hansen Sandseter, and Leif Edward Kennair, "Children's Risky Play from an Evolutionary Perspective: The Anti-phobic Effects of Thrilling Experiences," *Evolutionary Psychology* 9, no. 2 (2011): 257–284.

14. Deena Prichep, "To Raise Confident, Independent Kids, Some Parents Are Trying to 'Let Grow,'" *National Public Radio*, September 3, 2018.

15. A map of U.S. neglect laws is available at the Let Grow Project website: https://letgrow.org/resources/state-policy-maps.

16. Cartoon by Sophia Wiedeman, "I can never tell if I'm allowing independent play or just ignoring her," *New Yorker*, February 15 and 22, 2021.

17. Jessica McCrory Calarco, "'Free Range' Parenting's Unfair Double Standard," *The Atlantic*, April 3, 2018.

Chapter 9

1. Stephen James and David Thomas, *Wild Things: The Art of Nurturing Boys* (Carol Stream, IL: Tyndale House Publishers, 2009).

2. Euan A. Ashley, "Towards Precision Medicine," *Nature Reviews Genetics* 17 (2016): 507–522.

3. See https://obamawhitehouse.archives.gov/the-Press-Office/2015/01/30/Fact-Sheet-President-Obama-S-Precision-Medicine-Initiative.

4. In the interest of full disclosure, Xenia has always done all the kids' nail-clipping in our home.

Epilogue

1. Jennifer Traig, *Act Natural: A Cultural History of Misadventures in Parenting* (New York: Ecco, 2019). Chapter 1, entitled "Look Busy" and subtitled "On Outsourcing," surveys allo-parenting from the days of ancient Rome (infant abandonment) to modern times (parents sticking their littles ones in front of a TV or a tablet). For Traig, the history of parenting can be boiled down to mothers and fathers, throughout time, searching to do *as little as possible* parenting.

2. Tweet from Kimberly Harrington (@honeystaysuper), since deleted.

3. Chloe I. Clooney, "The Parents Are Not All Right," *Medium*, April 5, 2020, https://gen.medium.com/parents-are-not-ok-66ab2a3e42d9.

4. Farhad Manjoo, "Two Parents. Two Kids. Two Jobs. No Child Care," *New York Times*, April 22, 2020.

5. Rachel L. Harris and Lisa Tarchak, eds., "I Have Given Up: Parenting in Quarantine," *New York Times*, May 13, 2020.

6. Kelly Fradin, *Parenting in a Pandemic: How to Help Your Family Through COVID-19* (self-pub., 2020).

7. Michelle Goldberg, "Who Can Endure the Loneliness Required of This Moment?," *New York Times*, December 21, 2020.

8. Tweet from Matthew Segal (@segalmr), January 1, 2021.

Index